TRANSFORMATIONS OF THE SUN

122 passages on finding new life after loss

Transformations
OF
The Sun

122 passages on finding
new life after loss

Dr. BethAnne K.W.

GOLDEN DRAGONFLY PRESS
AMHERST, MASSACHUSETTS
2018

FIRST PRINT EDITION, August 2018
FIRST EBOOK EDITION, August 2018

Cover illustration by BethAnne K.W.
Copyright © 2018 by BethAnne Kapansky Wright.

First published in the United States of America
by Golden Dragonfly Press, 2018.

ISBN-13: 978-1-7325772-1-3
ISBN-10: 1-7325772-1-8

Library of Congress Control Number: 2018953497

www.goldendragonflypress.com

CONTENTS

vi

For Dad.
Who always said,
"Every day is a good day,
just some are better
than others."

Forwards and Onwards

WHEN I FIRST wrote *Lamentations of The Sea*, I intended for it to be a book of comfort and a friend to those going through grief. Writing it was not only an act of catharsis and healing, but it was a way to organize, sort through, and make sense of the grief journey I undertook when I lost my brother, Brent, in January of 2016.

At the time, I never imagined I would go on to write a sequel, but as you'll see in the following pages, there was always more to the story than what I told in the first book. When I finished this manuscript and sat back to take in the whole scope of these pages, all I could think is: *Girl. This is a brave book.* It took a lot of courage to get to a space of its telling, but it's time, these words have become a wildfire burning in my soul asking to be released.

In the same style as the first, *Transformations of The Sun* is composed of a variety of passages that can be read in order or that can be read by simply finding a passage that feels good for your heart on any given day. This collection of poetry, prose, personal essays, meditations and reflections shines light on a range of topics including grief, loss, transformation, identity, reinvention, spirituality, the afterlife, and all sorts of other beauties and complexities of being human.

Grief will change us. We don't get to go back to the person we were before the loss and that is a loss in and of itself. But grief can also be a gateway. A door to a bigger version of self. A catalyst and metamorphosis of beauty and deeper transformation. An invitation to bigger growth and authenticity. A testament to the changing power of Love, which truly does endure eternal.

I hope I've captured some of that in the pages of this book and that you find something here that sparks your spirit and offers your soul nourishment, healing, and hope.

Love,
BethAnne

UP NORTH
Saying Goodbye to Myself

Goodbyes can be painful, this can be true, but we will never find new hellos if we can't release the space of who we used to be.

1

WATCHTOWERS OF LOVE

PERHAPS ONE OF the cruelest truths that comes with loss is that you can't return to who you were before. You can't crawl back into your old shell of self. You can't rewind to a reality where your loved one is still here; because you are constantly reminded that your life has definitively changed. And with that change, you will be forced to change as well.

There is no road map for who you become after grief. There is no right or wrong or *go this way* or *don't do that.* Those of us who've passed through grief's wasteland and found ourselves on new shore know that each step forward will be a step into something new and different than who we were before. We also know that we'll be called back into that wasteland from time to time, and so there are new undercurrents in our rivers directing our flow, which didn't exist before; our river is forever changed.

Sometimes the change is more subtle: something internal has shifted, invisible to the naked eye, only perceived perhaps by your own felt-sense of innermost rearrangement. Sometimes the change is more visible: something tangible and external, where you change part of your life because you find as you move forward after loss that there are parts of your life which no longer fit who you've become. Most times it is both: an internal rearrangement that manifests by making changes to your external world.

It's the kind of change that can be incredibly lonely, nobody can bear the burden of this change but you. And yet that change also holds the potential for new possibility. That change can strip us of all that isn't real. It makes us realize our priorities. It urges us to do the things we want to do now and not later— *because we have learned that there may not always be a later.*

But mostly that change holds the spark of new life if we can learn to fan the flame.

It may not be the life we would have chosen, but we have also learned the power of grace when we were in the wasteland, and so we try to accept that this is the life we've been given. And since we've also learned from our loss that life is an infinitely precious gift not to be taken for granted—we try not to take our own life for granted. It is in this space of gratitude where we can transform that spark into a blaze, and become a brighter light than who we were before.

The kind of light who learns to see the sacred in every day. Who decides to use their own light to try and warm the world. Who takes the pieces from the wreckage of their grief, builds a watchtower of love out of them, and then shines the fires of their love-light so bright and high it is visible for miles and miles.

Reaching out to others who feel lost and alone in the dark, helping them begin to see the path to find their way home.

2

INFINITY

It was just a flash of time
—you and I—
those younger years of
bunk beds and donald duck
and butterflies and let's pretend
and holding hands out in
the summer's rain.

Puddles to ponds to lakes
to seas,
we grew big and knew
what is love,
what is change,
what is pain.

Last year I crawled across
the desert for you my friend,
searching, seeking, hoping—
trying to find
your end
(goodbye Brent)
never again.

New Begin.

They say Life has rhythms
all its own,
but they don't make sense
sometimes…
the tide doesn't always ebb with the flow
and the sun doesn't always rise with the set.

And you were supposed
to be HERE now,
but you're not—
and now I'm tasked
to not forget.

Come walk with me
and hold my hand
(invisible though you may be)
for I spy you in a billion stars,
sense your name on the whippings of the breeze,
find your face in the change of the rains of these days

And though you're no longer
here for me to see:
I hear,
I feel,
I receive,
I believe—

My brother, you fly with infinity.

3

*Faith is having vision
in the absence
of sight.*

4

SPIRIT

"You have to believe it first. Not wait until you see it first, then touch it, then believe it… You have to say it from the heart."

—WALLACE BLACK ELK, LAKOTA

T HE FIRST TIME I heard from my brother after he passed was on a beach in Hanalei. I was empty, lost, bereft in heart, and a complete contrast to the sunshine and balmy waves of island ease going on around me. I'd learned of his passing only 24 hours before, and I was staring at the waves of the ocean, thinking of all that had transpired in that time when very clearly his voice was there and it simply said, *Little Sister—take good care of Mom and Dad. You're all they have left.*

Then like that he was gone, I could almost feel his energy going *up, up, up,* heading to someplace well beyond me, well beyond that golden sand.

The next time he came to me was a few days later while I was sitting on his favorite beach, MacArthur Park, intentionally trying to see if I could sense him. It took me a while. At first, I was trying to sense him as he was here on earth, and then it occurred to me that his spirit was now infinitely bigger than who he was here. He wasn't Earth Brent; he was Spirit Brent. Which meant he was now Love and Peace, Compassion and Forgiveness. *Now a part of the light.*

Then I sensed him. He came to me like a surfer in my mind's eye—I could feel him out on the ocean riding the waves in euphoria. Whooping, laughing, and sounding joyful in a way he had never sounded in this life. It isn't that he wasn't present before and then all of the sudden he appeared, it is more like he'd been there the entire time, and once I shifted and changed how I was trying to sense him, I was able to. Like trying to tune into a radio station and finally finding the right frequency.

After that, I began to sense him often. He was at his own memorial, I didn't feel him until after I had delivered the eulogy; but as I sat back down shaking, quaking, and choked up, I could feel him in my mind. He made jokes during the sermon and pulled at my hair like he was tugging on a pigtail, leaving me with a sense of gratitude and *thank you* for the service and all that was done to honor him that day.

A few times in those first few months, he had messages for me to give to Mom and Dad. Sometimes he had messages for me. Sometimes it felt really clear—as if a text would appear in my brain that hadn't existed before the words popped up, and it was unmistakably him. At times, it was more of a felt-sense that he was nearby. Other times he felt far away, especially when I was in the thickest part of my grief. But even when I couldn't fully sense him, I knew he was out there.

It was like a gorgeous new musical sound had been introduced into my stream of consciousness that I'd never heard before, and once I heard it, I couldn't unhear or forget it. And it made it easier to listen for it then hear it again.

Believing was never an issue for me, I just did. I know Brent for Brent. I was far enough along on my spiritual journey to know you don't have to see something to have it be real, what is most real can only be seen with the heart, and the heart's eyesight is different than the eyes. Spirit speaks to us all the time, it's just that we don't often recognize it as we have expectations of how it should look, so we sometimes miss what is right in front of us trying to get our attention.

At the time, I wanted so badly to be more open about Brent, but I believed I would be discounted. It's not that I thought people would think I was crazy, not if they actually know me, it's more that I thought they would believe my mind was tricking me. That I couldn't handle my own grief and my loss of Brent, and so I fabricated and created these imaginings in order to offer myself a false sense of comfort.

But I believed in my heart they were real. Like I said, he was my brother, we were born so close together his presence has always been a part of my life. I know Brent for Brent.

Knowing that Brent was often close and having an ongoing connection with him didn't necessarily alleviate my grief or the emotional gutters I had to crawl through on my grief journey, but it did bring comfort. Especially on the days where I sensed him most strongly, my grief would abate for a time, and I couldn't help but be filled with the overwhelming sense of love, joy, and peace he now radiated. Usually, that high feeling would last throughout the day, and then I would wake up the next morning and return again to wherever I found myself in grief land.

They say those we lose rarely leave without leaving a gift behind, and I noticed that during this time something else started to happen as well. I started to have a massive amount of spiritual and intuitive growth. I began to sense and perceive things I didn't before. I began to hear things in my mind and heart that felt like deep spiritual wisdoms and truths. I sensed worlds I couldn't see, but I could *feel* them.

As open-hearted as I am, this was uncharted space, and sometimes I would doubt it—the human mind often wants to reject as fancy what it can't see or understand. But then signs and symbols would show up: certain songs, hearts in the clouds, rainbows, lucky pennies—all things which held a special meaning between me and Brent, and I couldn't deny the timing of the synchronicities. Even though I couldn't see him, it felt like Brent was standing right in front of me, waving his hands, trying to get my attention and tell me *this is all real*, and that all I needed to do is *stay open and believe.*

I traversed two journeys in 2016. My grief journey and my spiritual journey. Both of them were invisible. Both of them happened inside of me. Both of them were hard to talk about at the time. Both of them were difficult and beautiful, confusing and altering. I changed in that year in ways that nobody could see, and yet those changes began to fundamentally shape and set me on a new course in my life.

A paradigm shift happens when I realize the unseen world is as real as this one, and I begin to learn to make space for both. To better clear my mind so I can hear. To learn how to listen and see with my heart. To learn discernment and accuracy in what I sense. To learn how to receive. To learn my own nature and my own ability; sometimes I am better able to perceive than others, so I learn about my capacities and my limitations.

I realize that the pictures, images, and perceptions that have flashed in my mind since I was a child are actually spiritual gifts. I learn to work with Spirit and better refine these gifts. I learn to ask questions about my own soul journey and receive information through pictures, resonance, words, and a deep sense of knowing. I get brave and slowly begin using these gifts to work with others, and some of what comes out of that is so beautiful and life-changing, I know beyond a shadow of a doubt I've just claimed a birthright: I was born to do this work.

I can feel Brent at my back, urging me on, telling me to stay open, stay brave, stay on the path, no matter what anybody else thinks.

I grieve and I grow. I contract and expand. I become bigger, even as I'm absolutely humbled by all that is taking place. I feel Spirit hollowing me out so I can hold more space for Love. I cry in my mentor's office telling her I don't want these gifts, I just want my brother back. She gently reassures me it was never a trade, it wasn't my gifts for him, I was always meant to walk this path. I know this truth in my heart, but I believe these things would have happened further down the road, and I don't believe I would have arrived where I am at, at 39 years, if not for Brent.

Some days I walk around with so much love in me, I feel like I'm crackling with it. It is impossible to work with Spirit and not be filled with a profound sense of divine love and light. Sometimes, I see the soul instead of the person, and it's as if everybody glows, and I can feel how unconditionally and absolutely loved we are. Sometimes I get faint impressions of gossamer webs of grace that feel like they are weaving all of this and all of us together. I'm undone in these moments of transcendence.

It changes me. All of it. My grief. My transformation. Brent. Spirit. The gifts. The invisible school I attend as I learn to work these things out within myself. The knowledge that even though we may sometimes feel alone, we are never alone. We are so supported by Spirit and Love in ways we can't even conceive.

I don't pretend to understand all of it, and I can't even begin to fathom it. I see glimpses of what I know is a massive, amazing, divine whole. At times, I feel like I've fallen into a giant library in the starry ether. There is so much knowledge and wisdom packed in there; it feels so grand, and I feel so small. Love is what holds this space together, so much Unconditional Love.

And so sometimes, I don't try and see any pictures or ask any questions: I just set my frequency to love; set my intent for truth, grace, and light; say a special prayer as my way of dialing up; and then sit and breathe in the sacred presence of the energy of Love that exists here. Every now and then when I'm in this space, I sense Brent extra close by. It's like we're in Rumi's Field. A place that exists out beyond the ideas of rightdoing and wrongdoing when the world is too full to talk about.

Our souls fly together through the stars, and he meets me there.

5

CLARION CALL

I BELIEVE MY SOUL tried to prepare me for the loss of my brother, and all the changes that would domino afterward, long before it happened. Life and our soul paths weave an intricate dance, where our own rumblings and shakings and tremors begin to take place within—alerting us to a premonition that change is coming—even before the actual earthquake will occur.

It's hard to pinpoint the exact time my own rumblings started. My husband's entry into my life was certainly a start; his move to Alaska in 2014 and our beginnings of a life together only built on that. I started to have a wistful sense of *wouldn't it be nice to build a new, fresh life where we both had to start over? Together.*

The rumblings started to get deeper after our wedding in November of 2015. We married and honeymooned in Oregon, and for the first time that I could remember, I wasn't excited to return home. *There's nothing there for you anymore*, a voice inside me said. We returned and a restlessness came over me that was only exacerbated by the claustrophobic dark of Alaska in December. I had a growing sense of emotional, psychological, and somatic awareness where I felt like I was trapped in a box.

Going into 2016 those rumblings turned to tiny shakes. I had the inexplicable urge to dye my light hair dark or trade my usual rainbow wardrobe in for black—I think I wanted to shake things up, make people look at me differently, break some mold I had unwittingly created for myself that no longer fit. I had a deepening sense of spiritual presence and awareness that wanted to grow, yet I was so busy with all of my obligations I had little room to explore what that meant, other than through small bursts of poetry and prose in my quiet writing moments.

Then Brent passed and the real earthquake arrived. Grief shook and shook and shook the foundations I had built my life upon. My world cracked open. Fissures rose up inside of me. Some of my old contents of self fell through. I was forced on a grief journey that ejected me out of my current life path and unceremoniously deposited me elsewhere.

It was in this space that all those rumblings and tremors that had pre-existed and forewarned of change started to make more sense. I realized I wasn't truly being the person I felt called to be. I realized I had a store of spiritual and intuitive gifts trying to expand and grow, with not enough space to do so. I realized that as long as I was in Anchorage, I couldn't shift the paradigm of myself. I realized the truth of my words, *there's nothing here for you anymore*, on a deeper soulful level. Those words were my clarion call that I had a purpose I was not fulfilling, one which I wasn't going to be able to fulfill in my current life.

My soul was trying to tell me something, my heart trying to give me courage to move in a new direction. Brent became my biggest cheerleader and biggest reason to go—he had never made it past year 39, and now I was in my 39th year with a terrible knowledge of how drastically short life could be. I could feel something inside of me, pulling and calling and tugging and pushing. Compelling. *You cannot stay, you have to go.*

And so we made the decision to move to Kauai. We set a date, and as 2016 turned into 2017, I prepared to step into the year where I was going to make a break from life as I knew it and go answer the call of my soul.

6

Unmet Self

I cannot stay, she said.
I must go be somewhere, something
some other else.

I cannot stay, she said.
Or I will lose this precious seed
I must go plant—
And never meet my unmet self.

7

BIRDS OF PARADISE

A WARM SUN RISING, viridian plants waving, birds singing 100 different songs; it is our last morning on the island.

This year our annual visit is drastically different than the year before. The year before is January 2016 when we received the news of Brent; the year before is a year of brokenness and grief and small tinges of gratitude that we are together to comfort one another, as we prepare to return to Alaska and face the overwhelming tasks of death.

The year before, I was only beginning to take the first few steps of my grief journey. I had an impending sense of knowledge that I was about to climb a terrible mountain, and I knew my heart was big enough for the task, but I didn't want to be anywhere near that mountain. The year before, I had no idea how hard it was going to be and what it was going to feel like to have to return to Anchorage, say goodbye to my brother, carry on my practice, hold space for so much and so many, even as I traversed the tumultuous terrain of grief.

This year it's February 2017, and things have changed. We just passed the anniversary of Brent's loss a few weeks back, and the grief feels different: it's still present, but there is also so much love that now exists in that space. This year we flew over to the island with the knowledge we will be moving here in the summer. This year I'm about to climb a new mountain, but it's not terrible like the last one. This one will be arduous—moving to an island will not be light work— but unlike last year's unfathomable mountain of grief, I know what is waiting on the side of this one.

Kauai.

I went to bed last night feeling nourished and content and woke up at 4 a.m. feeling overwhelmed. It hit me all at once that this is the last time I will stay at my parent's condo for a vacation because we will soon be living here. And then I was hit by the scope of what getting here will entail. I don't look forward to all the work there is to do in actually selling a house, closing my practice, and preparing for a move over the next 4 months.

It's time though. Times have changed, and I changed with them. A slow rearranging of life's tides reshaping my shores. Then all at once in the blink of an eye. Personal evolution can be a hard thing to measure, but I've traveled well beyond the bounds of who I was last year.

I can see the outline of a new life here. It's just enough of a structure to feel there are some lines and parameters to give me a sense of guidance and direction, but with enough gaps and blanks to give me plenty of space to create something new.

I feel bolder here. Like the birds of paradise unfurling their orange and purple plumes outside the front door, there is something unfurling inside me that feels freer and liberated. I find myself having the courage to start writing about more metaphysical and spiritual matters and my experiences with those, especially in relation to my brother. My inner artist is beginning to stir and says she's looking forward to creating in this space.

Mostly though, I can feel a visceral, tangible sense of untapped possibility waiting here. Like I will be given a blank canvas and get to create of it whatever I desire.

That blank canvas is just around the corner, but for now, I'll be flying back to Anchorage for the last time to see to the tasks of sorting, releasing, goodbyes, moving. It's going to be a lot to close down a life, but when you compare that to where things were a year ago, it doesn't feel quite so overwhelming. Besides, this last year has taught me that no goodbye is truly permanent. They are doorways for hellos in new forms. Always something waiting on the other side, and those who are most important to us, those we've loved best, always find a way to meet us at the door.

Even if they now exist in the beyond.

I sat outside on the lanai last night with my father talking about Brent. Dad has discovered the hard truth that the year mark only denotes that a year has passed, it doesn't magically make the pain less.

Can you better sense him over here Dad?

I ask, because it is so easy for me to perceive him in this place, sometimes in more concrete ways when he makes his presence known, sometimes just as an energetic imprint when I can feel he's close by and far away and everywhere all at once.

Dad thoughtfully considers, then shakes his head. *No.*

We're hard-wired very different Dad and I. He's concrete and practical, while I'm intuitive and expansive. He doesn't see or feel or experience the way I do; I don't organize, plan, and focus on exact details the way he does. But still, we are bound by the same heritage and since I so often feel Brent, I am curious if he can sense him too.

After a slight pause, he reconsiders his no and says, *I can see him here BethAnne. It's so easy to imagine him here, to visualize him in the places he loved. I keep half expecting him to come walking up this path.*

I tell him to take comfort in that. That that *is* its own form of seeing. Then we sit in silence and watch the sky change from rose to dusk to twilight. The wind hollers and whistles with laughter and breath. The faintest flicks of stars begin to shine. An uncanny peace descends as night falls and everything is still and well and calm.

You can almost hear a presence, coming on up the path, past those blooming birds of paradise, going round the corner and through the door.

I can't wait to see what's waiting on the other side.

8

DECONSTRUCTION

Y OU CAN'T BEGIN a new life without letting go of an old one. If you try to skip that process, you will often find your old life follows you into the new, still trying to finish itself.

Deconstruction can be a painful thing. Taking a life apart is psychologically disorienting, displacing, and dissonant. It will make you feel like you don't know where you belong and like a wrecking ball has been taken to your world, yet deconstruction is often necessary for completion and closure. For it is only in deconstructing the foundation of an old life and identity that we will find the space and the ability to reconstruct something new.

I go into Spring of 2017 knowing I am about to take life apart as I know it. That most of the main structures I've built my life upon— job, home, geographic location, community—are going to be dismantled and no longer exist as they once did by the time I am done. Change often isn't linear or intentional, losing Brent sure wasn't, that was forced change where life swung its wrecking ball into the structures of my and my family's life. *And so there is something strangely satisfying about the idea that this time I will be the one swinging the wrecking ball.*

Even though I know it's going to be challenging and hard, and I'm completely overwhelmed by the monumental tasks that will need to be accomplished to move to an island, I am also grateful I'll be able to live the change. Process pieces as we go through them. Say my goodbyes. Go to last places. Have time to reflect and reconcile myself with the changes taking place. *It is a gift in its own way, even though I know I may not appreciate that gift while going through it.*

Losing Brent has given me perspective though. He was ripped so abruptly from me, without time to process the pieces or say goodbye; I didn't get a vote in what happened. Yet leaving Alaska is my choice, and I have now lived and internalized the truth that everything in life is transient, and so there is something empowering about knowing

19

that I am the agent of change when it comes to the matter of my own geographical transience. *I am choosing this; it's my choice.*

Life is a dance of giving and receiving. Action and yielding. Holding and releasing. There is truth to be found in all. Sometimes we deconstruct life and sometimes life deconstructs us: both sides of the coin are needed if we are to become who we are meant to be in this world. Last year, life took me apart and helped reform me into something new. This year? Now it's my turn.

9

WEATHER PATTERNS

THESE DAYS I am learning radical lessons on self-compassion. That being whole is a paradigm shift where we don't see parts of ourselves as good or bad, just different aspects of being human. That kindness towards our experience of self is the gateway to peace and acceptance.

These days I can't get enough of the cold spring sky who asks me to come sit beneath her and tell her of my cares for a while.

These days my insides are consumed with continental drift, having traveled far from where they once formed; I've changed. The shifts and skiffs and schisms inside defy words. One day over there. Now right here. And I couldn't tell you how I arrived except to say that heart and guts and the courage to dive for my truth became my brave bateaus.

These days shedding old skins, clearing out stuff, and a continued unraveling of my life have become daily goals and occurrences, even while life's winds continue their constant blow without regard for my loss of layers. Their ongoing gusts whip wearing bones.

These days—the other day—I forgot my brother was no longer here. *Isn't that silly,?* I thought as I went to text him, blinking, remembering: *He's been gone over a year, there's nobody at the end of that phone.* I wondered at the mind's ability to forget.

These days my heart finds new ways to break, and I leave trails of crumbs wherever I go.

These days I write of my shades of self without purpose or determination or organization; just honesty, disintegration, disorganization, reinvention, revelation.

These days I can't get enough of that cold spring sky who asks me to come sit beneath her and tell her of my cares for a while.

She promises there is warmth on the horizon and an easier breeze coming soon. She tells me about the story of her life; the constant weather patterns she must flow, change, adapt, contain, hold.

She tells me like sky, like life. Sometimes it aches to become.

10

STRESS AND STARDUST

I HAVE HAD MY head bent in, looking down instead of up.
This season in life has me twisting into spirals, and not the good
kind where you drop into your truth and go deeper into your own
knowing. More the game of twister kind, which leaves you upended
on yourself as your right foot tries to stay on the red dot while your
fingertips grasp to touch the green.

You fall unceremoniously, like there's no tomorrow, except tomorrow
is coming—sooner than you think. And you'll shake your mat of dots
out into the breeze, redistribute, recycle, rehome colorful bits of yourself
that were not meant to stick, so your mat is white, your canvas blank,
with space for new shapes and shades and selves.

I've been trying to sit in peace and talk to the stars this season;
untwist long enough to remember my place; find my way back to my
core of grace. It's not that Spirit is silent, it's just that sometimes I can't
hear my own thoughts over the rush of steps running through my brain.

Today I hear, I receive, I see. I *see* myself in a sea of white, a trans-
lucent, rectangle board dividing my brain. The symbolism's simple,
the image jarring though not unkind. I see how my mind is simply
split among too much, too many, divided in attention; my thoughts
stuffed with obligation and stress and closed cotton restriction, and I
understand why I can't *see* right now.

I *see* how I'm going to make it through the next few months of
busy, chaos, relocation, release. With my wooden sword and 3 heart
containers, I will be like Zelda—going from world to world, level
to level, castle to castle, chipping away at challenge after challenge,
one obstacle then the next. Slowly knocking them out, leveling up,
until there is nothing left but an empty home, an empty office, and a
one-way ticket to a new time zone.

I *see* myself flying like a bird. Migration is coming, but before I
go South I must be here in the North, or I'll miss important parts of
my journey.

And then I *see* him. He's been terribly quiet these weeks, absent in my need. But today Brent blows light at me. Sprinkles of star and white and peace and clean. *Chin up Stargirl, chin up. You're doing just fine.*

For the first time in weeks I'm looking up, I'm dialing up, I'm listening up. And I see this season in life for what it is. Just a season, it will not always be. I sit under that cloud of stars, complete in their dust.

Find what I need to start chipping away at the next level.

11

DISPLACEMENT

PSYCHOLOGICALLY, DISPLACEMENT IS a terribly confusing place to be. It leaves you feeling like you lost your place in line, and you're not quite sure where you now fit. Do you go to the back of the line? Do you try and cut back in? Do you start a new line?

I think it is impossible to go through loss and not have a sense of displacement. After Brent, I had that sense of losing my place in line; not because people stopped caring about me, but because I had to step out of line a while and go find myself, and by the time I returned to the line I realized it had changed. Life had spun on around me, I'd lost a lot of time wandering through grief land, new people had shown up in line, and the intensity of the journey I had come through no longer matched its direction.

And that was perhaps even more jolting—I had changed. Changed in invisible ways nobody could see or fully understand. How could they understand what I had barely begun to grasp myself? Those changes left me feeling disenfranchised. Not quite part of things the way I used to be, no longer sure where my parts did fit.

How do you learn to swim when there's no water nearby? Or learn to fly if nobody teaches you how to use your wings? Or learn to paint if you were put into baseball instead, and you don't even know that taking an art class is an option?

I was searching for something, something that wasn't available in my current mold of life, I couldn't say what, except some part inside was trying to grow and couldn't do it in my old lines. There were days that I missed my old lines. I missed having a sense of certitude for not just where I fit but how. *I didn't want to swim or grow new wings or have whatever it was that happened to me happen.*

I missed the old me, even as I knew I couldn't force myself to crawl back into that space.

Displacement chafed and left me wandering outside those lines, looking for a space I could call home. Home was no longer going to be Alaska; as difficult as it was to imagine the finality of leaving, everything took on a transient, temporal feel. But home was not yet Kauai, and I knew that even when we got there, it would take a while to find my place.

There are times we remain displaced. Making a temporary home in the nebula of in-between. Knowing that for everything unforming something new is reforming. Knowing that gesticulation is a process, incubation sometimes necessary for something inside ourselves to grow. Acknowledging the extreme discomfort of this space.

Acknowledging the necessity of this discomfort, for comfort is enticing and often hard to release, and we would never find the motivation to change and expand if not pushed past the comfortable limits of who we used to be.

12

In Between

No longer that person
I used to be,
not quite the one I'm
stepping into,
I find myself somewhere
in between.

Broken,
but not irreparably damaged,
I slowly unwrap, unlace, unbind
the more I let go, the more I heal,
and the more I heal, the more I find
myself free to grieve—

What was lost
what's been found
who I was
who I'll be.

The new moon
peers out against her own darkness,
dance of shadow, dance of light;
I stare at her black,
in transition like she—

Then let myself free fall
into my own change,
unforming
reforming
transforming
and then again—
until my feet find new ground
with new pieces of me.

13

How Soon is Now

G OING THROUGH THE items in your home and making choices about what to keep and what to release is a walk down memory lane where you revisit old versions of yourself, remembering just who and what you were about when that particular object joined your collective.

These last few weeks I've sorted through so many past versions of me, it's been dizzying.

It's fairly easy to trace my steps and evolution up to the point of 2016—I've smiled fondly at some of those older memories then kindly said goodbye, as I don't believe they are meant to move to Kauai with me. But the course trajectory changed entirely the day my brother died, and I continue to live the truth that you cannot lose somebody you have deeply loved and not become a different creature.

Some days I am still unable to wrap my mind around him being gone, and I have this profound awareness that I don't really know who I've been or how I've managed to do life these last 15 months. I just know that something was altered on a foundational level January 18, 2016. I walk around with something invisible broken. Nobody can really see it. Sometimes I try and tell others about it—dare them to *see* beyond what is being presented to them, *see* deep into me, see if they can *see* and validate the scope of this wound.

But words fall flat. And not many people have been taught how to *see*. And I still don't fully have language to describe the break, so I can never convey its profundity. I can feel it though—it's gone into hiding, burrowed far within, because it's never truly had space or time or support to come out and breathe and be seen.

I have come to the conclusion that it is the kind of broken wound that can't be healed by others. Instead, it must be offered up for healing to the land and sky and trees and seas and source of love itself.

There is magic in the earth of Kauai. Geologically the oldest of all the islands, something mystical is contained in its soil—sacred stories and ancient ways and a reverence for the land that has been lost by too many. I don't believe it is a mistake that the place that serendipitously opened up for us to live is up in the hills of the Wailua Valley where the first inhabitants of the island lived.

There is healing and support of a kind I've yet to experience waiting there. I can feel it in my bones. I can feel it in my mind and heart and soul. That broken part of me has been stirring in hope at the prospect of space and sky and breath and safe and calm that is coming her way. *Soon, soon, soon*, I tell her, even as I keep asking her to stay invisible and stay deep so she doesn't disrupt my flow, and the rest of me can keep showing up and getting on with the tasks of moving and living and going forward.

Maybe someday, when the shores of Kauai can be called *home* and not just *dream*, enough space and time will have traveled by that, I can look back on the changes that losing Brent wrought within, see the bigger picture, and better understand how and perhaps *why* this current version of self came to be.

But for today, I have an office to pare down and sort. A coat closet to clean and clear. More boxes filled with stuff to take to donation. Rays of sun that are shining through the windows asking me to take a break for a bit, go be with the trails and trees and find respite in the earth of Alaska, slowly waking up to the seeds of spring.

And a wistful yearning for ancient hills and melodic seas and a cauterized wound in need of ocean salt and sunshine continuing to call to me.

Soon, I tell her. *Soon, soon, soon.*

14

FISHBOWL

I float, a flake of fish food.
A drop of sustenance in a hungry bowl.

They come one at a time taking nibbles out of me.
Bite by bit by bit by bite.
Some so tiny you'd barely notice,
but even tiny bites add up.

Translucent and fading,
I drift in the water trying to hang on to my scraps.
Realizing:

There is not enough of me
to go around.

15

THE EMPATH'S LAMENT

EMPATHS HAVE A hard time with the word *no*. Usually, we *see* a need, we *feel* the need, and we get pulled in. For myself, it is an impossibility at times not to be drawn into somebody else's energy, to feel what they feel and see the world from their perspective. I've become so good at making energetic space for others, I do it unwittingly without a second thought.

It's who I am. I step into the energy of another person, I mold and bend to that energy. Shape shift to fit their shape, involuntary reflect and mirror back what I see, and hold space for their reality. I can't help but be understanding and compassionate, because I see the world through their lens. This makes me say *yes* even more; I can't seem to stymy my own energy flow from pouring out into a void of *need*.

This has resulted in too many *yeses* across the years. *Yes, I can do that. Yes, I'll go. Yes, I can help. Yes, I can stay late. Yes, let's try and see when we can fit it into our schedules.*

Yes binds my ankles and hands, pulling me under: I've been drowning in a sea of voluntary consent for years, with nobody to blame but me.

What I wish to be, would like to be, want to learn to be after 40 years of *yesses*, is the kind of woman who simply says *No*.

I want to learn to honor the holiness of the word *No*. *No* is an act of self-love. *No* is the gatekeeper that separates where others end and I begin. *No* is a boundary that helps me respect my time, my energy, my thoughts, my emotions, my being. Saying *no* is simply a *yes* to myself, for there are places inside of me that can't be found when I am with others and doing other things. They can only be found in the pristine promise of silence and solitude, where I learn to shine the mirror I hold for others into myself.

Empathy can be an incredible gift, yet sometimes it feels like a double-edged sword. And as such, I need to learn to better direct and wield it, instead of cutting myself upon it much of the time. In fact,

I'm coming to see and believe there will be times when I need to lay that sword down entirely, so I'm not even tempted to use it. For it's grown rusty and worn from overuse, and I'd like to learn to use new tools that can only be discovered by retreating into myself.

After many years of *Yes*, I am finally coming to see: *No* is the key to freeing my heart, my energy, my mind, my time, so I can fully assent to something inside of me.

16

THE SOUND OF SILENCE

I wonder how long
it would take,
if I were still and quiet—
(no talking,
or listening,
to anything other
than the sounds
of the birds
and the breeze
and my heart)
to become bored and
miss word's starts

and ends
and in-betweens
and conversations with others
and exchanges of meaning
and people stimulating
and connections relating
and dialogues vibrating

but for now,
too much contact
has become overwhelming
and draining,
and I yearn
(in my
introvert,
introspect
soul)
for the sound of silence

and a nervous system that's
whole

and calm
and hush
and peace,
and a brain with space to roam,
free from noise and energy leaks

I believe in the deep,
which calls in my sleep,
I would find what I need
to return to my home,
go inside
my own breath,
my own space,
my own bones

in my heart,
the thunder would roll
(*shhh! listen!*
can you hear its
vast roam?)
shaking and quaking
with truths unknown,
and I'd listen alone,
in silence,
and know:

I belong to the sounds
of my soul.

17

BREAKING OUT

I T CAN BE hard to break your own mold. We get stuck in shapes that no longer suit, but we've held them so long we don't know how to break away from our old version of self. We create pockets and parcels where we try to make space for something new to come out, but sometimes it is still not enough space.

Sometimes something drastic is needed, because we find despite our best intentions of trying to pop ourselves out, we fall back into the cookie cutter shapes we have imposed upon ourselves, along with the ones others have come to expect of us. But most molds are meant to be broken after a time. They are only useful to hold us in stasis and space so long as we find their shapes useful and in congruence with the shape we feel called to be in this world.

Sometimes our shape changes, and our mold doesn't.

So we have to make a new one. Become the shaker and changer and breaker of our own shape. No matter how messy. No matter how difficult. No matter how tiring. No matter, no matter. Because when our soul calls for growth we have to learn to break out of the old, so we can free ourselves and find the space we need to begin to create the new.

18

Hidden Gems

THE HOUSE IS fairly still and quiet this morning. In the background, The Eagles are encouraging me to take it to the limit one more time, and I'm stealing a moment of calm and beauty from the frenzied pace of the last few weeks. Potential buyers will be here to look at the house in 2 hours, and if they don't make an offer, it gets listed Monday.

So many changes. The last few weeks have been head spinning, and I am finding it is impossible to not feel displaced as life is in contraction, expansion, transition, transformation. I don't quite belong here anymore, yet I'm still not over there. And so I find myself in the unstructured, uncertain space of between.

Most days I wish I could just be on the other side of things. Safely tucked into our new home in Kauai, up in that green jungle, playing 70's music on a balmy Saturday with strong coffee and large measures of lazy. All goodbyes would be said, the chore of packing and moving done, the animals adjusted to a new home, and myself finally sinking into a new skin and pace of life.

But just like with my worst of grief over Brent's death—when I so badly wished that I could skip forward 6 months and be through the pain, only to find hidden gems of light and lessons of soul buried among the muddy layers of grief—I am finding that there are all sorts of hidden gems and lessons of soul tucked inside the layers of these chaotic days of change.

The gem of space.

The more stuff we get rid of, the more I don't want to be owned by stuff anymore. I want to have room to live simpler, cleaner, smaller, so I have more space to expand and live life bigger.

The gem of a slow loosening and letting go of attachments.

I've been integrating on a deeper level that it is okay to let go of what people think. Unless it is a person who has habitually shown up with a life saver and helping hand when I've been floundering and going under in life, I've never felt so free or unconcerned about others or their perceptions, opinions, and perspectives of my journey. Or given myself so much permission to empty my life of all but the few I hold closest to me.

The gem of balance.

I've been lopsided for a long time, my energy output not equaling my energy input. I've been trying to right that after years of over-giving and finally realizing—I am not the emotional custodian of other people's spaces. Progress has been made in this area of my life, but I still see a time soon coming where saying *no* becomes my default setting, so I have space to finally, fully, freely say *yes* to something in me.

The gem of change. The gem of capability. The gem of release.

The gem of deconstruction—dozens of other gems in dozens of other ways. Too many to write about, except to say the biggest gem that is glowing brighter and brighter, a diamond of light in this messy transformation, is the gem of reinvention.

I was at a class the other night surrounded by other therapists in the trauma community, faces I've seen and known for years. We were going around the room introducing ourselves and saying what we specialized in, and when it got to me, I said: *My name is BethAnne Kapansky Wright, I'm a psychologist in private practice for two more months. Then I'm moving to Kauai, and I'm going to reinvent myself.*

You've never met a more supportive group than a room of trauma therapists, so these words were greeted with warm smiles, surprise, and kindness.

Somebody asked, *What will you do when you get there?*

I have no idea, I said. *I don't know, and I guess I'll find out.*

Saying these words, looking back over my shoulder at all it's taken to get to this point, finding new resolve to keep going and releasing the reigns—

I have never felt so free.

19

DOORWAYS AND STORIES

W HAT WOULD IT be like if we were taught that death is just a door and that we don't have to close it after somebody has passed? What would it be like if we lived in a culture that understood how to keep that door open, who valued and respected what was on the other side, and who thought it was perfectly normal to have communication from time to time with those we love who've moved beyond.

Some cultures are taught that wisdom from the beginning, yet western culture doesn't contain these teachings. It's not often talked about, and it's not something normalized in our collective consciousness, and so it isn't something that is particularly accepted and valued in the mainstream—let alone seen as healthy and normal.

What would it be like if people didn't look at you like you were daft when you said that you'd heard from your brother? Or that you believe the signs and symbols you've started to see everywhere are his way of communicating with you.

What would it be like to consider that supernatural phenomenon is actually just natural phenomenon, and it is us who've made it something other than what it is, relegating that territory to psychics and mystics and new agers and seekers. Making it seem as if it is something to be divined, or something way "out there," or worse yet, something to be feared.

What would it be like if it was socially and culturally acceptable to talk about our spiritual experiences in real, visceral ways with curiosity, openness, and love? What would it be like if somebody else didn't interpret it for you or project their beliefs onto you or shut you down, and instead encouraged you to stay open to the beautiful love that you feel streaming through?

What would it be like if such experiences and stories were approached with open hearts and open minds? What would it be like to be able to sincerely tell people, *my brother still talks to me, and the other night I saw him in my mind's eye and he looked like an ebullient, blazing, star-being surfing through the sky.*

37

I can only imagine. I don't know what it is like, and I don't feel that freedom.

These experiences have become things that I have to hide in the closet every time company comes over. Or if I choose to take them out, I have to decorate them—throw a slipcover on and fluff up, so it looks somewhat else than what it really is. I don't have the space to fully express my experience, and I can't find many judgment-free zones. And since nobody has ever taught me the vocabulary or language of what I'm experiencing, I don't know that I fully have the right words to share—even when I do find safe spaces.

I am alone trying to understand and learn a language my brother seems to be trying to teach me, trying to expand my mind in such a way that I can knock down the barriers in it that keep me from perceiving. Trying to discern and open my heart in such a way that I can better learn to listen.

This leaves me walking around bearing untold stories. If grief is a taboo, talking about one's encounters with the spirit world and my dead brother feels even more of a taboo. So I've got a double dose of taboo: I am crumbling in my pain over Brent, even as I am in awe of the miracle of who I sense him becoming on the other side.

I find the stories inside of me beautiful, but also heavy with a growing sense of gravity and urgency. They begin to push down on me, hard, as they ask to be released and told. I re-realize over and over I cannot be the person I am meant to be in Alaska; I have no place to put these stories in this space. My life here doesn't support these stories. I don't even know if I'm allowed to let the woman who wants to tell the stories out: *who would believe, see, value, and listen?*

So I retreat into my world of introversion and writing to try to put words to my experiences instead. I try and tell them through bits and pieces of poetry. I write *Lamentations of The Sea* and discover that in so doing, I build a beautiful memorial for my grief, and as other eyes read the words I become aware that I am no longer alone in the grief part of my story. I try and couch some of my interactions with Brent into the words; metaphors and imagery that is real, yet could be taken as imaginative prose. I hide the new language I'm learning among the language of grief I am beginning to speak quite well.

I tell my stories to nature. She becomes my most faithful witness and listener. I whisper them to the kind trees in fall on morning walks along frosty trails. I trace them into the grace of freshly fallen winter snow. I smile them into the budding leaves and bright blooms that begin to decorate spring. I talk to the clouds, the sun, the sky, and the nearby lakes as often as I can:

My brother's soul is so beautiful, I say.

We know, we know, my dear one, we know, they softly answer back.

I seek places with others who may be more like-minded. I go to a full moon ceremony up in Manitoba, Canada. I sit in a sweat lodge tucked in an unassuming backyard in Anchorage. I help assist in a shaman's circle with a group of graduate students; and when I finally say, *"My name is BethAnne and I work and channel with the unseen world, and I still feel and see my brother on the other side,"* it is a blessed relief, and I realize how at home I feel in this circle where there is finally space and curiosity for my words.

I become humbly grateful for the bits and pieces of Native traditions and teaching I've learned under my mentor and in ceremony. It gives me a framework and a space to put something that nothing else offers. It helps to acknowledge and validate the importance and realness of my experience and the stories I'm holding within. It encourages me to own my truth and keep living it.

But mostly, I work on believing in myself. On reminding myself that everything I am experiencing is genuine and valid. And I begin to see moving to Kauai as a massive act of self-love and a phenomenal promise that I will go a place with space for these stories to begin to be lived and breathed and told, because I've begun to realize that even though some of this language feels new to me, it is the oldest language in the world.

It is the language that began everything, and the same language that binds us together still. It is the language that guides and nurtures and protects. It is the language that birthed our origins and holds our future; it is the language we all return to when our time on earth is at an end, and we find ourselves stepping through the doorway, beginning a new story.

It is the language of Love.

20

Goodbye in Dreams

They keep coming to me
in dreams.
Faces of times gone by,
places of yesterday.

Kindness on their face,
even those who did
the most disgrace,
have apology in their gaze.

As if to tell me—
go and be well
and leave behind
the ghosts of this space.

Things are kinder
in dreamland.

Conversations occur
that wouldn't take place
in the cognizance of day
where barriers
and images
and the distilled drift of time...
all bring a distance
not easily
erased.

But what may come in dreams?
Where love can be the frequency
and we leave behind our egos

and shells of physicality.
And let our minds meet,
while spirits greet,
and our soul's
forgive
and mend
and entreat.

Wrapping up my loose ends
into complete,
I keep hearing those ghosts
so clearly—

I'm sorry.
Godspeed.
Now go in peace.

21

CHRISTMAS ORNAMENTS

IT'S A GRAY Saturday with a cool early June sky, and I have a difficult chore to get done. I've been putting off the task of going through our Christmas decorations. I don't want to remember the grief in the boxes or take the trips down memory lane that will inevitably come: *Brent is tangled up in all of those memories. How do I go about choosing what to take and what to leave behind?*

I didn't even bring them out at Christmas. I put the decorations away after Christmas 2015, but I left the tree up, decorating it with hearts for Valentine's Day as I found its presence and light comforting in the dark of an Alaskan winter. Then Brent died and the tree stayed up through the spring. By the time I had the energy to think of taking it down it was already July. So I chose to put cloth flowers on it to celebrate summer; cloth flowers became pine cones and red leaves for the fall, which were traded for anything shiny and tinsel-like that I could find around the house to nestle in its branches for Christmas 2016.

I couldn't bring myself to decorate that year; the weight of what was in those boxes felt too cumbersome. The loss of a first Christmas without my brother and the memory that the last time I'd seen him was Christmas Eve of 2015 pressed heavy upon my mind. *Those boxes feel thick with old memory and grief, and I don't want to acknowledge what is in them.*

Today it still feels like an onerous task, and I'm weary and tired from other onerous tasks related to the physical and emotional labor necessary for this move. But this is something I've put off until the end, and since we are getting down to the wire, it's time I drag out the two big red tubs with the emerald green lids and get ready for the process of sorting.

Our little fluffy dog, Frodo, bounds into the room. It's as if he intuitively senses I'm in need of joy and cheer, and he's determined to keep things on the bright side. It works, as I can't help but laugh at his fascination while I pull ornament after ornament out of the boxes, as he sniffs among them thinking they are toys for him. He picks a stuffed Santa to start chewing on, and I don't have the heart to take it away; his happy energy is too comforting and heartwarming.

Tiers of memories are in those ornaments. I slowly take them out and make myself look at each and every thing. The wooden soldiers and stuffed teddy bears of childhood. Traditional figurines and a snowman collection from early adulthood. The fluorescent pink bulbs and turquoise elves from my post-divorce years when I was feeling down about my first single Christmas, and so I reinvented it with neon, glitter, and feathers.

And last, the ornaments my husband and I bought on our honeymoon in Rainbow, Oregon where we delightedly discovered a treasure of a Christmas store and spent an afternoon picking out eclectic decorations that felt like *us*. Happy ghosts. A giraffe. One fuchsia flamingo. A parrot. A white dog popping out of a pumpkin that looks like our sweet, old Sam.

Almost 40 years of life is told in those ornaments, so much is bittersweet. And then Brent is there, I feel him. He is light in motion and he gives me pictures of all the possessions and stuff he left behind when he left the earthly realm. *If I could let all of it go, Little Sis, so can you, so can you. It's only stuff, and you're not going to find me in stuff. So only take what brings you joy, Sis. Only take what brings you joy.*

His words free something in me, and my perspective shifts—I truly don't need to take much of it with me.

So I lovingly pack up everything, thank it with a smile for serving so well for so many Christmases, and wish all of it well in new homes with families who need it more than me. I take a large shoebox and fill it with the ornaments we bought on our honeymoon, a selection of those single year neon glitter bulbs, and a few other meaningful pieces. Come what will be, our future tree is going to be looked at with happiness. Not with objects that hold any sadness or regret or the bittersweet of memories.

I already have enough bittersweet. I'll take my tree with joy, please. I close the lid on the box, smiling. Imagining that the next time it is opened will be in a new home, on an island. In a space that has felt so terribly far away, but is drawing nearer and nearer. *Where the words Mele Kalikimaka will be the thing to say on a bright Hawaiian Christmas day.*

22

In Living Rearrangement

L IFE RIGHT NOW is a rush of change.
So many pieces of myself have been tumbling down so fast, I find myself feeling self-preserving, wanting to pull them into me, examine them and say goodbye before sharing those examinations and goodbyes with others.

I didn't know what it would be like to lose one life to gain another. How hard it would be to take the whole of all I own down to quarters and fifths and pints and eighths of a shipping container. Or how freeing it would be to let go and discover just how many things one can live without. I don't always know who or where or what I've been these last few weeks.

It has struck me, on a fundamental, makes by bones quake and reverberate kind of level, just how much of myself I've given out, poured out, spent out throughout the years. It is in the make-up of a people-helping job to be a giver, and it is in the nature of being a healer to heal. While I don't know the exact equation that equals the balance of energy output vs. input when you feel called to give and heal in this wanting world—I know my equation is way off balance and that I have wanting inside my own world.

For any of us, the best we can do is just try to be ourselves and figure out life as we go along. And when we figure out something isn't working—change it.

It has been a massive change making the decision to leave the state and then taking the steps to get there. Perhaps more massive than others can realize, because they are not the one embodying and holding that experience within themselves and feeling the full felt-sense of the internal shifts and changing places and rearrangements that I've been feeling within; this move isn't just about change of address, it is about change of identity.

But there is something in me that has been trying to break free for quite some time, and this is the only way I could figure to find space to let her breathe and be and evolve. This week I whispered to the clouds and the sky and the trees in fervid gasps of blessed frenzy—*I quit, I quit, I quit.*

I cannot be this version of self any longer. I will not be this version of self any longer.

It is both terrifying and liberating when we realize we have reached the end of something inside of ourselves, and we find the courage to start living our lives in such a way as to align with that truth. Greater alignment always equals change. And change is hard. But necessary for growth, because we did not come here to stay stagnant.

So here, in living rearrangement, is where I find myself. Examining my tumbling pieces, 6 weeks out from what is the biggest move of my life. Liberated, terrified, exhausted, electrified. Wondering just who I will be in 6 months, as I try and get a sense and glimpse of the face of the woman I'll become.

Whoever she is, she's learned the holy power of the word *no*, and she's not afraid to save herself.

23

THE TEARS THEY COME

THE TEARS THEY come in waves. Salty and salient, free floating down my face.

It's the season of goodbyes, and I'm feeling the change on the days I'm not too numb and tired from this life transition. May was for saying goodbye to the house as it went up on the market and went into contract; I spent time in each of its rainbow rooms gently enjoying soft moments of stillness, acknowledging all this space has meant to me.

June is for goodbye to friends. Those last dinners and brunches and times together are happening *now*, and I find myself taking more soft moments for each face I'm seeing and thinking about exactly who and what and how they have been in my life, and what we've brought to each other throughout the years.

And July is for Alaska. We will be in Kauai by the second week, and with just a handful of days left, my husband and I agreed to make no more commitments or plans with people when the month begins, so we can set aside those days to find soft moments for ourselves and this great state in the midst of this move.

I'd like to drive in the sunshine down the Turnagain Arm one last time. Go up into the mountains and spot the little pink flowers tucked in the tundra. Walk the dogs by the duckpond. Breathe with the trees. And if there's no time or energy left for any of these things, I'll just sit on my front porch and reach out in my mind and thank this space for being my friend and containing me all these years; let my thoughts drift to those mountains and trees and seas and green.

We don't have to physically be somewhere to connect with it, and the same holds true for the people we keep in our hearts.

The tears they come in waves. Silent and silty tracing rivulets down the tired cheeks of my face.

My brother taught me how to let go. That you don't have to be with somebody to still *be* with them. That separation is but an illusion, connection our destination, love an invitation to learn to love beyond the physicality of time and space.

His birthday would have been yesterday, he would have been 41 this year. I can feel him nearby as I run through the forest, tugging at the pigtails in my mind, whispering with the winds of vicissitude. I reach up and give the trees high fives; they speak with him and the breeze in trinity telling me how close I am to the finish line.

Almost done with who I was, almost ready for who I'll become; I can't contain the depths of my own space, and I let myself spill out onto the steadfast embrace of the earth, *and the tears they come in waves.*

24

SEED OF POSSIBILITY

WHAT WOULD ANY of us dare to do if—even if scary and farfetched—we believed it was possible?

Because all dreams that come to fruition start with a seed of possibility. And we either nourish or starve that seed by the ingredients we feed it.

We have to cradle those seeds, blowing wishes and hopes and *yes you cans* into that dream. We have to believe in our own vision of self. So very, very badly that we refuse to let anything get in the way. Refuse to take doubt and fear for an answer when faith and hope will better suffice. Refuse to believe that our dreams are anything but entirely possible.

Because all that composes our realities, at some point, was no more than the faintest wisp of a dream. A seed of possibility. And their creation falls to the only ones who can see them through to fruition—you and me.

25

RISE

LIFE THESE PAST few weeks has been all about saying goodbye to myself, even as I can feel myself sinking into a new hello.

Seems like I've been writing about moving to Kauai for over a year, and now we are 2 weeks away. I find it surreal and strange and beautiful to be experiencing the change instead of thinking, imagining, and writing about the change.

The change is now, and my chambers echo with its certainty.

There is a last round of farewells this week. My practice closes in 3 days. The house is getting emptier and emptier, and it's as if with every letting go I find myself lighter and lighter, the murky, grueling plod of the past few months changing to a swift upward sprint towards the sun and light.

Manifesting this move has required downward gazing—carefully watching the path in front of me, anticipating any obstacle and challenge that may come up, and adjusting my steps accordingly. But now I find that we are close enough to the end that I am looking up with a profound sense of awe and near completion.

I said I would get to Kauai, and I am doing it.

I can feel something loosening inside of me, waving her jubilant octopus arms, rolling with the mermaids of the deep, and getting ready to *move* in a way she hasn't ever had space to. I laid in bed this morning talking to the ocean then cast my thoughts out into the trade winds, sending messages of *aloha* and *greetings* to the island along their fragrant streams.

Gratitude swims strong and true; I fly with birds of rainbow in my mind; somewhere inside of me a woman is poised to lift her wings and begin to rise. Soaring into newness of being.

26

OCEAN SONGS

I T'S LIKE A still silent hush came over my office.

My suitemates synchronistically gone this week; the incessant clang of construction going on outside mysteriously muted. I found myself alone with one last handful of clients. Moving in a year's time became 6 month's time became 3 months became 3 weeks became my last day, yesterday, after more than a decade in my practice.

So many goodbyes, so many years tied up in that office; I sat at day's end at the heavy wood desk that's now gone on to donation, and said *goodbye* in solitude. Not knowing what to feel or how to feel, and so I just thanked the space for holding me and so many stories for over 10 years.

Letting go can be a painful truth. Undoing in its dissolution; freeing in its resolution. I've walked around these last 4 weeks in Anchorage, and all I can feel is the sands shifting inside of me, sweeping back and forth as they shake their old patterns loose and begin to rearrange into a bigger sense of self.

If you would have told me a few years back that I would close my practice, I wouldn't have believed you; I had too much tied up into it and was fearful of losing my stability and financial security blanket.

And now I can tell you that it wasn't my circumstances that shifted, which allowed me to let go—truth be told I have no idea what I'm going to do for money—it was simply my perspective that changed based on a deepening desire to put faith into action and live the words of truth I have been writing for so many years:

The universe will support you and make a way when you follow your soul's path.

I feel called to go to Kauai, and so I'm going. Trusting it will somehow all work itself out. Which is how I found myself sitting in that hushed office last night reflecting on everything that has transpired all my years in private practice.

It is our full that makes us whole, and so I let myself be in my own fullness of emotion and let the relief and release and grief and freaked out and deep breaths of authenticity wash in and out like the not so distant ocean I am swiftly heading towards. Completely alone in my emptied space, reflecting on all that has passed.

Feeling my ocean sing within. I turn the lights out. Satisfied.

27

THE DUCK POND

It was 5 years ago when I walked around the duck pond
with my youth and our gremlin dog.
Drinking coffee, feeding crumbs to the geese.
My world is safe, small, content. Clouded with judgment
and fears and a tiny wisp inside who wonders, more.
I'm not sure if I notice the sky above,
I am in the only box I know.

It was 4 years ago when I walked around the duck pond.
My more found herself lost in a green-eyed vortex that
played a wicked game of chess with my naive heart.
I don't know where to find my lost pieces so I walk along
searching for them among the calm waters and happy feathers.
I plead with the sky above, I am breaking.

It was 3 years ago when I walked around the duck pond.
I am broken and whole. Unboxed.
My wisp has become a flame burning through all that isn't real,
it consumes much. My youth looks at me, confusion in his gaze.
I have few answers, I wish I knew the questions.
I have $1,000 in my pocket, a fist of broken dreams and the love
of a gremlin dog who licks the salt from night's sorrowful waves.
I look up at the sky above, *I wonder why life has brought me here?*

It was 2 years ago when I walked around the duck pond.
I have spent a year meeting parts of myself I never knew existed.
Some are dark and shaded, some are free and live,
all are beautiful. I realize I am learning how to love.
I smile at the sky above, my insides match my outside.

It was 1 year ago when I walked around the duck pond.

I can still feel the bruises and scars left by his careless prints.
Desolate, my heart plays a familiar song of break,
so I play myself broken once more. I walk along
searching for my pieces among the calm waters and happy feathers.
I accuse the sky above, *nobody told me having*
a brave heart would cost so dear.

It was 6 months ago when I walked around the duck pond.
My gremlin dog is dying, and my youth comes to say goodbye
to this precious link to our other life and space.
We have lived different answers, but time brings peace to our gaze.
My most faithful friend can no longer walk, so I carry him around
one last time and sing him to sleep across the horizon.
I know how to carry:
I have become a woman who has learned to carry her full.
The water has never been so calm. I cry with the sky above,
I am sad and wise and very strong.

It was 3 months ago when I walked around the duck pond.
He put his arm around me for the first time. We had met
on a trail in Oregon a few days after I sang my friend to rest,
talking faithfully since. I showed him all my brokenness
that makes me lovely and whole, then he crossed the ocean for me.
We watch February's sun lay against Winter's ice.
He feels warm and safe and good.
I wonder at the sky above, my heart knows profound gratitude.

Today I walked around the duck pond.
A white ball of fur chases sunbeams at my feet,
fascinated by geese, joy in motion. I think about the man
moving across the water for me, this time staying for keeps.
My heart is massive and open and deeply brave.
Filled with happy feathers and calm waters.
I laugh with the sky above, the only box I know is love.
It has no walls.

For the last time, I walked around the duck pond.

It has been 3 years since I wrote the words above.
In that time, a brother gone; a life undone; a reckoning begun;
an unraveled self begets a journey of belief and brave that
calls me to new space.
A wet ball of fur keeps time with my feet,
the rain drops, and I say goodbye to all, goodbye to these days.
My heart brightens at the thought of home—
where now one man, two dogs,
one calico cat stays.
Soon a trip across the ocean where a new life abides,
waiting to be claimed.

I reach up and touch the sky above, He reaches back,
brushes my face. The ducks swim in merry medley,
I breathe in healing, exhale grace. Then leave in peace
with the lessons of this pond in my heart,
because I have now lived the truth of this place—

You will never lose what you hold in your heart:
Our Love endures eternal.

28

Tides

LIFE HAS A way of moving us along. Crissing and crossing us. Sometimes towards one another and sometimes apart; the siphoning of apart usually being more painful and stretching than the connectivity and receptivity of towards. But we are not meant to stay the same throughout our timelines and neither are our relationships.

For relationships, like life, like ourselves, are fluid, dynamic, and subject to growth.

It can be difficult to experience these changes in a relationship; sometimes downright heart ripping and mind splitting. I often think about my brother and how abruptly he was taken from me with no warning that there was going to be a sudden irreversible departure of presence and that I would be left to make peace with something totally unpeaceable.

But I have come to realize over and over in the almost year and a half since his loss that it is possible to make peace and accept something that feels unacceptable—if you just make a little space to accept the fact that part of it will never feel okay. And this is the crux of letting go—you have to learn to make space for your whole experience of self in the matter.

Sadness. Regret. Reminiscence. Good Memories. Anger. Confusion. Wishes that it was different. The realization it is not. The pain of separation and the echo of a felt-sense of belonging. The light and the dark. The love and the hate.

The only way I know to embrace change is by learning to embrace the whole of who we are. We can't learn to let go if we are turning a blind eye to, or willfully engaging in denial of part of ourselves, which is like trying to run a race with a broken leg—you aren't going to get very far. And we can't let go of somebody we have loved, whatever the nature of that love, if we don't acknowledge the part of ourselves that wants to hang on.

Sometimes the best we can do is take the hand of the part of self who wants to stay and stick, gently say with the utmost of care—*there, there my dear one, I know this space was beautiful in its time, but there is no life for you here anymore*—then help that part of our self continue to learn how to turn their face towards the light of what is ahead.

Such is the paradoxical nature of change. You can't fight the tide of life. Nor were we meant to, for no matter how resistant our minds may feel, it is in the nature of our soul to reach for change.

We have a way of seeking expansion, even when we don't always know what we are seeking. And Life has a way of moving us along.

29

HERE AT THE END OF ALL THINGS

THERE'S NOT MUCH left in the house. A red couch and a bed that donation is coming to get tomorrow. Some blankets and two camping chairs. Our luggage. A giant green dumpster is sitting in our driveway, we've been steadily filling it all weekend in order to finish clearing the space.

I'm on the red couch in an otherwise empty room along with the fur beings—Frodo, Sam, and Shire—feeling a bit like the real Sam and Frodo after they cast the ring into Mt. Doom and the mountain erupts destroying everything. They find safety on a giant slab of a rock, surveying the void of destruction around them, and Frodo says to Sam, "I am glad you are here with me. Here at the end of all things…"

I feel that end. I've lived it this last week where I've walked through a haze of a surreal reality, surrounded with the knowledge that I am doing something I will only do one time in my life. The whole thing almost feels like an out of body experience, so strange and unprecedented it is to be breathing in this space of change. I've thought about the last day for a while, and now it's upon us and it feels otherworldly as I think about all the "lasts," all the "final moments" that have transpired.

I will never say these final goodbyes again. I will never see some of the faces I've said goodbye to again. I won't climb these same mountains, drive south on the Seward Highway on a perfect bluebird day, camp in Seward or walk the spit of Homer. I will never drive to my office or go to my favorite coffee stand or sandwich shop for a moment of sanity during the workday. I will never come home to this home after one more day. I will never run these same trails or talk to these same trees or occupy any of the spaces that have held me in their stead during my years in Anchorage.

I will never see my childhood home again. My parents plan on putting it on the market and moving to Kauai full time in the fall, and so last night was a final goodbye. Dad cooked way too much as usual.

We ate gooey enchiladas and spicy burritos and watched fun movies. And I tried to memorize that sense of "one last time," remembering many evenings such as this where we all banded together after Brent passed, finding comfort in the ritual of delicious food and good flicks.

I walked throughout and around the house in leave-taking. The rain poured down on the windows, and I sat on the old red carpet in the playroom one last time and let my tears pour with it. I knew goodbye wouldn't be easy, but I'm taken aback at the intensity of the moment as I think about the number of leave-takings one takes within a life.

It's a lot to take in. Too much really. And I can feel that I will have some processing to do when I get to Kauai, as my emotions are backlogged and jammed up, and the stress of leaving is beginning to weigh heavy. I've been holding it together all these months, but I can feel a burgeoning sense of extreme anxiety as I consider how flying from Anchorage to Seattle to Kauai, with 2 dogs and a cat, is actually going to look.

We took a moment of respite earlier in the week using the 4th of July as a reason to still ourselves and go climb a mountain, knowing we probably wouldn't have another opportunity. Rainbow Peak is gray and cloudy and beautiful as always. The tree lined trail gradually breaking way to steep shale, higher and higher through craggy rocks, tundra, and a terrain that can only be described as *Alaska*.

I tried to take it all in and embody the moment in its entirety. Saying all my final thank you's to the land. She's given me so many gifts throughout the years, and she's sheltered and supported and comforted me through so many shells of self. I try to be with the mountain that day and just have gratitude for the simple pleasure of visiting her one last time, contemplating all the change.

Now as I sit here on my red couch in my almost empty room, I can say that after going through all the steps that got me from *thinking about change* to *living the change* that I have lived the truth that our dreams are not impossible, if we believe in them and are prepared to do the work and stay committed to their completion.

I've fed the hungry belly of this dream for the past year. Telling myself it was possible. Telling myself, despite the fears and complications and logistics of getting there—*we will get there.* And now *there* is almost *here.*

It's a day for goodbyes, and so I take one last run along my beloved trails, knowing tomorrow we fly out, knowing this is yet another last. There is a strange hush and sacred silence as my feet cover familiar terrain. An uncanny awareness as I try and fully drink in every moment of this last. The flowers seem brighter. The cheerful puffs of clouds against the clarity of sky's blue make music. Even the dilapidated neighborhood I run through takes on a nostalgic tint.

The final part of the run is under a long canopy of trees. I've talked to these trees, I've given countless fistfuls of tobacco to these trees with whispered prayers of hope and gratitude. They are my friends, and I will miss their familiar faces. Amber eyes and chocolate bark and verdant visage. And then I hear it in my heart, it's so soft you might miss it if you didn't know to listen.

Farewell, farewell, farewell, they say.

A soft breeze begins to play, and I notice they wave their leaves in *adieu* as the sun makes kaleidoscopic patterns of light through the arches of their branches. Some of them reach down, extend a limb, and brush my upstretched hands; it is a holy moment, and one that requires me to slow down and walk. I feel their benediction and a blessing all at the same time. And I have nothing to offer except the tears streaming down my face and *thank you, thank you, thank you.*

Thank you for this final goodbye. Here at the end of all things.

30

PARTING WORDS

My dear girl—
you thought
it was over,
but you were just
getting started.

Coming home
to your self,
slipping into those
wings you sewed
from faith
and fall
and fortitude.

Preparing to fly
so high,
the sky is no
longer your
limit:
up,
up,
up
into the stars
where those
who've walked
before reside,
and your
destiny lays.

Like a tree
you shall be;

roots firmly grounded
in this blessed
earth;
she is big enough
to hold your days,
treat her kind
and you'll
always find
your way.

With limbs
outreached,
and mind
outstretched
your wanting branches
waving free,
your wise eyes
bravely see:
soaring through
the galaxies,
collecting Love
for you and me.

May you be safe.
May you be well.
May you be the change
you seek.

Go forth
my friend and shine
your bright;
and be the light
you're called
to be.

DUE SOUTH
Living the Dream

*Dreams, like anything else, often look very different
in the living than in the dreaming, and so like
any truth we find in dream time,
require a bit of shape-shifting and adaptability
in order to make sense of them.*

31

SKY WALTZ

IT'S HARD TO believe we're here.

I woke up to a purring kitty; we laid side by side on my pillow, chins resting on hands and paws; watching the jungle light go from deep night green to dawn light moss to malachite daybreak. A few roosters wandered by, a feral cat, too many birds to count; Shire's eyes widened into saucers as she watched and wondered at this new space.

Transplanting to Kauai was nothing but difficulty and work and living the sweaty hard truth that if you want something different in your life, you have to make it happen. I find my mind flashing back to the bizarre quality of our last day in Anchorage, as if I was moving through a dream:

What it felt like to walk away from the house and know I'd never see it again or call it home.

The soft patch of forget me nots that bid me not to forget on our last walk around the neighborhood.

The complete surreality of getting into Dad's car, heading to the airport, and driving down Northern Lights Boulevard for the final time.

Flying out over a full moon with two confused dogs and one terrified cat as I wept from emotional release, relief, and something else I couldn't name.

After airports and layovers and the time warp of travel, we arrived on the island 18 hours later in a stressed out heap of wrinkled exhaustion. Sweat peeling off of us in our new found space of humidity, and an even bigger sense of dreamy surreality that we were actually here.

But we are *here*. I woke up trying to wrap my mind around a new truth: we now live on one of the most beautiful islands in the South Pacific. Today is the first day of a new book.

Like the cat, my eyes become saucers on the morning walk. Keen, aware, heightened with an acute sense of awakening and opening. I talk to the plants and marvel at their red and yellow and fuchsia leaves. Watch the sky waltz a triple step of cloud and light and shadow. I waltz along with two dogs and a heart in awe.

I wonder why it took me so long to get here even though it couldn't have happened any sooner. Our new home feels so warm and welcoming, and I think about the steps that brought me here. The path was straight and sure—charging ahead with resolution—with little room for missteps or looking back or regrets. Because without that kind of resolve, I wouldn't have found what I needed to let go of life and all I loved in Alaska.

But here, on this island of *Aloha* there is room for so much more than I've wakened to before. And under an ever shifting skyscape, with an earth so drenched in the spirits of those who came before I already hear then beckoning me and whispering in my mind—

Now it's time to dance.

32

WORLDS WITHIN WORLDS

They said:
why would you want
to move to an island,
won't you get tired of not
having more space?

But what they don't know
is that there is a world
of secrets within each stone;
a million stories told through
earth's kind trees.

A new sky-star symphony
every softened eve;
the wisdom of the ancestors
if you listen and believe.
Wind-speak on the breeze;
truth and knowledge in the sea—

A person could spend
their entire life learning
the truth of a bird's breath,
and learn what they need
to be complete.

And as awakening of day
calls me open with
rain's clarity,
light's majesty,
green's verity,
Kauai's mysteries—

I know a million
worlds of secrets
within my island of self,
(worlds within worlds)
and I believe and I see:

I will have all the space I need.

33

LADY

I T IS A sense of being dislocated and coming home all at the same time. It's day 3 in Kauai, and the sun is beaming up here in the hills where we are tucked into our new home in the jungle. The cat is watching birds fly by outside my office window, while some sort of chili pepper red flower waves in the breeze, and shadow mixes with light on the cloudy peaks above.

I've finally landed from my leap of faith, and though I'm still finding my firm footing and next step, I know I've landed where I'm supposed to be.

I can hear the air singing, the jungle's seeped in mystery, and my heart is beating slower than it has in a long time; I go out onto the grass every evening, press my palms to the earth, and offer tobacco in thanks to express my gratitude to everyone and everything and every force that came together to bring me to this magical space. I felt for sure the bamboo heard my heart the other night, as it clacked and clanked and swayed 20 feet high in receptivity.

It takes courage to trust our hearts. To make breaks from the past. To forge a new trail that we can't quite see. To trust that if we have the courage to follow what is calling to us, something better is waiting on the other side.

And to know that life will make a way for that which calls, but it doesn't mean that we don't still have to show up and do the hard work of getting there.

Yesterday I spoke with a woman at a furniture store named Lady who has been here for almost 40 years. "If you came to this island with an open heart, a sense of joy, a love for the earth and the sea, if you let the island teach you and don't seek to change it, you are in the right place," she said. "Only certain people are called to live here. But if you are here seeking money, seeking materialism, seeking to change the ways, to change the island, it will bid you leave this place."

We chatted for an hour. I bought a wooden stand needed to help organize our space. She asked my opinion on whether or not her place was feng shui, and we talked about how the most valuable gifts in life cannot be measured on a piece of paper but are only found in the heart.

Last night I sat out on the lanai. Rain pouring down, deepening the sense of green. Thinking about Lady and what she said. *Teach me your ways*, I whispered to the breeze, heart open wide, humbly ready to receive. An orange butterfly circled free; a wild boar poked its head out of the jungle long enough to see me then retreat; and the bamboo swung and swayed and sighed in peaceful unity.

34

BREAK

WHAT DOES IT mean to live a life where we let ourselves break in the direction life is breaking us? To be certain, this is easier said than done. There is a reason the word "heart" usually prefaces the words "break." Our heart-wisdom is stronger and bigger than our mind-wisdom, which is why most of the time when we are broken in life, it is the heart that takes it the hardest.

Heart break is the hardest break to heal. Unlike a broken bone, which can be reset and realigned, the heart doesn't heal back into the same shape it did before it was broken. The grief changing work of self becomes an invisible process that those who've been broken go through. They journey onwards from the bitterest point of their loss as they process their pain and go in search of healing and perspective.

Breaking is painful. Yet it is part of life. And the bottom line to learning to break is that while we want to think we are the ones in control—in the past I have clung to situations until my nails bled and my knuckles turned white trying to keep change from running its course—the reality is that Life is bigger than us. There are times where we will be asked to yield to it.

We can't control our breaks. But we can choose what to do with our own pieces. I write these words with the self-knowledge that the only reason that I find myself in Kauai is because when life swung its wrecking ball into my wall and took my brother from me, I let myself break. Let myself crumble. Let myself take space to be a mess, and then let life fill me up with new pieces so I could be rearranged.

I let myself disintegrate and reintegrate and integrate, and I learned to trust the process, even when I didn't know where the process is taking me.

It's the best any of us can do. Follow our own personal process in the bigger process called Life. Allow our shells to be shattered when something shattering comes along. Trust life to help us put our pieces back together. Look for the hidden lights in the darkness that will help guide us along the path. Learn to release instead of cling. Find the courage to just keep showing up and trying to find the love.

Fight relentlessly for a free heart, which learns to transcend the break.

35

HEAT WAVES

Everything
slows down
in the heat...

Time loses its
rigorous edge;
sharp shores
melt
into pools of
calm calidity.

Ocean waves
wash all harsh
away...
a warm bath
of blue and
green and
aquamarine—

Somewhere in
their cooling
gaze, I
d i s s o l v e
lose my pace
of hectic haze.

And in the melt
salt bath of sea
I learn to float
still
peace
clean:

And be.

36

CLOUD SPEAK

I'M WRITING THESE words from a space of relief and release and reformation. Eleven days in. Though I'm still unformed as I settle, find my way, and stay open to the bigger soul question of *why was I called here*, it is ineluctably more delightful being on this side of things than it was unforming my life in Alaska.

I've sat by the ocean as much as I can; she sings, the sea, and I'm trying to learn her music. I made a new friend who invited me to try her fitness class, which left my abdominals so sore they still ache. I went back to work quarter-time, smiling at the pups who insist on being in the room still taking their responsibilities as therapy dogs seriously, lending their calm loyal energy as I do tele-therapy with a few remaining clients.

I showed up for a modern dance class where I squirmed and turned and curved along to drum beats and heat. Melted into pools of sweat trying to run in the hot and humid. Made grocery runs, a Costco trip, and all the other odds and ends you do when you are first setting up house.

Walked around Kapaa, visiting local shops, realizing I don't know anyone and they don't know me: I have no history here. A thought that leaves me feeling like a blank slate—lonely and void and ripe with the crest of possibility.

I sit on the lanai most mornings and evenings listening to my heart think and seek in the jungle green; listening to the stories of the trees; discerning the sounds in the breeze. *Be still, take this space, this time is for you,* they say. *You need to reset your nervous system, learn to be peace.* The palms and fronds wave in emerald harmony, I sigh in return.

Eleven days in, and I'm slipping back and forth between different skins of self; all of them me; none of them quite me; I came here for a new skin and it's still forming around me. I don't quite fit here yet, but then again, I'm not supposed to. It takes a while for any of us to find our place, our fit, our tribe, our next step. We answer our questions about being through the acts of our living.

But there is a deliciousness in searching for my answers. To not carrying so much weight; the weight of a brother gone; the weight of being the strong, stable, dependable one. Each day is a revelation of ocean salt and rainbow talk and cloud speak and remembering how to breathe.

Instead, I keep offering up all of these things to sky's reach. Watch the clouds form and reform and become again and again. Lose myself then find myself in their shifts and shapes; learn to breathe and be peace.

37

40th MANIFESTO

I T's JULY 27, and I'm now 40. It feels like a good number. I get to enter into a new decade with a shiny zero and a solid four in front of it. Four points equal a square with no weak points, so in numerology a four represents stability, security, structure, organization and home. It's an auspicious age for this new book of life.

I believe in trying to leave an age better than I found it, I think I did that with 39. I believe aging is a gift because it means we still get to be a participant in Life. I believe I have many feelings surrounding outliving my brother that I can't quite name. Brent was supposed to hit 40 first and beat me to it by a year. Now he remains forever 39 in my mind.

And I miss him.

I believe in trying to find gratitude for life. I believe it is a gift to be on Earth at this time. I believe even with all the struggles and pain that it is still a privilege to live and learn and love and breathe and be a part of humanity. As cliché as it sounds—I can't sophisticate it no matter how I try to package the words—I'm grateful for the gift of life. My gift of life. Our gift of life. This Earth's gift of life. *It's so infinitely precious and meant to be cherished.*

I believe in joy and pizza and beaches and dogs. I believe we all have an inner mermaid longing for the songs of the sea. I believe in finding the beauty each day, even if you have to look a little harder for it on some days. I believe in being an active participant in the process of life. I believe in reinvention. And I'm so profoundly grateful to be in a space of allowance where I can reinvent, dissolving the parts of me I no longer need to pack around and finding new parts to help me move through this 40th decade of life.

I believe aging is a gift; not everybody gets to. Brent forever changed that for me, as I know every step forward into my own lifespan is a step he'll never get to take, and there is bittersweet gratitude that comes from that. He is *there*, and I am *here*. But he reassures me he's doing quite well where he's at and that his life was exactly what it was supposed to be, and he's where he's meant to be.

And so am I. Living on. Loving on. Breathing on. Believing on. Saying hello to 40.

38

It's not that our grief will ever leave us.
It's just that over time, it learns to grow wings.

Sometimes those wings will still drop us down in descent
towards the deep and the dark and heart of the pain.

But other times those wings will help us transcend,
taking us up and beyond, so we can embody
the utter beauty and miracle that is this life.

39

I'M A RAINBOW TOO

I T'S STICKY OUTSIDE, the breeze is a welcome relief, and day is softly
changing into twilight. I'm at a movement class called "Flow," eyes
shut, swaying, and listening to Bob Marley sing, *sun is shining and the
weather is sweet, makes you want to move your dancing feet.*

I feel like I'm in another world, and in one sense I am. This
moment of dance and tropical warmth that embodies the sense of
expansive movement that exists on this island *is* a new world for me.
Even the dancing I'm doing here is different than anything I've done
before; I curve and turn and do weird things with my limbs that make
me feel like I'm a kid playing in pleasure, oblivious to anything else.

In this moment I revel in the newness, revel in the change, and
revel in the information I am actually here—on Kauai in this little
dance studio moving like the trees—and that this is my life. Most
of all I revel in what it feels like to have the space to be somebody
new. To be this girl at this moment in time, whoever she's turning
into, I'm so grateful for my existence in this space and the oppor-
tunity to explore.

After we've flowed and twirled and twisted and curled, the last
part of class is on the floor. On our backs, focusing on the breath,
feeling the energy of the body. I notice the orange streaks of sunset
that are peeking through the studio's window. Brent and love and light
are woven through each of them. Magic and wonder and mystery as
the words, *when the morning gathers the rainbow, want you to know that
I'm a rainbow too, I'm a rainbow too, I'm a rainbow too,* fill the space.

And I don't want to be anywhere else, but in this love, in this
space, on this floor watching peaches and tangelos stream across the
sky as guava pinks come out and begin to gather the stars. Feeling the
breeze of the ceiling fan on my face, feeling the happy dance of my
own heartbeat, feeling into the space of my own possibility.

40

THE POROUS HEART

I MISS MY BROTHER. It's more subtle than it once was; a quiet melt instead of a deep thaw. Shades and nuances that lend themselves to a sense of longing, even if I couldn't tell you exactly what I long for. Nostalgia. Another life. Something intangible, yet lit with home fires, that nobody else could ever see or understand.

Today I jumped puddles with him; 4 and 5 years old; Alaska in August; *rain, rain, rain, rain, rain.* We made a game of it while Dad worked on his '77 Chevy Suburban and Mom served delicatessen burritos for lunch. We giggled while we ate, and she taught us the meaning of the phrase "raining like cats and dogs."

Yesterday we sat in the stars, him and I. I left my home in Kauai for a while, traveled upwards, wondered at what it is like *up* and *out* and in the *other world*. He feels busy; a jovially bossy tour guide in the afterlife. I get a strong impression of him helping people cross over and reorient themselves *there*.

This morning his old car took myself and my husband and the pups to the beach. "Beastie" I call her, a gold '02 Durango that has seen more adventure with me behind the wheel than it did in his life. A year ago, I had just claimed his truck as mine. We initiated it by driving way on up a twisty semblance of an old mining road, packed with cold streams and shale boulders to go camp by a waterfall in Valdez, Alaska.

This year brings new terrain.

Run faster, swim in the ocean, go adventure, I hear him say. *Eat a slice of prime rib for me, be generous with the baked potato. Don't forget about dessert. Do all the things I can no longer do 'Lil Sis. Don't just do it for me, do it for you, cherish this gift.*

Cherish your life.

A bright rainbow hangs overhead, I stand by his car and stare. I wasn't supposed to be over here without him, but here is where I find myself. Sparkling waves, new terrain, oceans of change, and a porous heart—never meant for the shallows—still called to swim the deep.

Here is where I find myself.

Here is where I find myself.

41

THE BLUES UNSPEAK

STARLIGHT HANGS OVERHEAD; polka dots of brilliance in a sapphire sky. I'm reflecting on how grief is eternal but so is love, as I walk while the dog keeps time at my feet, and the gentle palms remind me in their endless wisdom: *grace is infinite.*

I've been in Kauai for 9 weeks. Some days are poetry in motion, some days are just a script of normal life that happens to be set by the sand and sea. All days I am grateful I am here, all days I am reaching up—*heart open wide*—ready to receive what is next.

Most days I get a response, some days the response is simply the crash of the sea.

There are things I miss about Alaska. People and faces. The way the tundra turns to cranberry dusk this time of year and the sunset becomes a golden pot of indolence. But I drove home to the beat of pink streaks, cotton clouds, blue skies and ocean cries this evening, and my brother kept time in the clouds, as I realized—*I'm not missing anything.*

Grief really never does leave you. It weeps secretly in quiet corners; hidden from sight until it's ready to emerge on its own volition, keeping time to a timetable all its own.

Blue ginger strums the blues singing soulfully along with the company of azul snapdragons and little bells; the flowers here know when to joy and when to cry with songs I cannot sing but whose tune resonates so true I know the sound of deepest empathy.

Grief transforms. It huffed and puffed and blew my house down in 2016, a deconstruction of self, a resurrection of soul. So it is fitting in 2017 that I am on this island: her soul beats so deep you can't help but keep time in her keep.

Foreign at first, this land is now my friend. Strange with wonder, the flowers continually teach me to speak their silent unspeak. The sky holds new lessons every day; the spirits of this place stay continually linked.

I *do* promise you—

The beauty you carry
inside your heart
will be the same love
that helps you carry on.

43

PENNIES

THERE ARE TWO sides to every coin, heads and tails, and yet it is the same coin, both sides encompassed in an endless circle binding them together. The further I go on my grief journey the more I am coming to see just how much it is all the same coin. My experience is a matter of perspective, what angle I'm perceiving the coin from day to day.

Brent sends me pennies all the time as a sign that everything is okay. I was actually given a penny the day before he left this earth; I'd had an unexpected urge earlier in the week to watch *Ghost*, then a few days later I was at the airport preparing to board, and just as *Unchained Melody* came on the radio, I looked down and saw a shiny penny at my feet.

For Luck.

After that, pennies started showing up everywhere, all the time. Since time isn't linear in the spirit world, I assume Brent sent me that penny the first time to prepare me, to try and reassure me it would all be okay, and to establish a means of connection between us that I would recognize.

And all is okay, even as it's not. I've become used to just accepting this contradiction as part of my reality. I wouldn't be who and what and where I am if not for Brent and all the gifts that came from his crossing over, and yet some days I am still shocked and grieved at who and what and where I am.

The collateral beauty that has come from my grief guides me, haunts me, directs me, saddens me, comforts me, reassures me, disconcerts me, darkens me, lights me and has become me. I miss him and I love him and I miss me and I love me and I miss us and I love us; I dance back and forth between the sides, circling round and round that coin as I remember love is endless.

I have come to see that grief is more than just sorrow and sadness and lamentation. It is beautiful and transcendent and transformative as well; the contrast of one side, sharpening and heightening the experience of the other. Two sides, one coin, endless in its cycles: both sides of equal value.

44

ISLAND LIFE

A s August's heat stretches high, melting into September's warm gaze, life takes on a new rhythm. Daybreak and moonlight walks become the norm. Shorts, tees, and no make-up my standard uniform. And I learn what it is to live in a place where sunshine and ocean are no longer a scarcity.

My days are slow and easy, though at times a little directionless compared to my Alaskan life. I'm grateful I'm still working with a handful of clients as it gives me just enough structure to have a sense of purpose, even as I start to consider the question of—*now what?*

The shipping company finally delivers our household items, and I'm relieved and gratified to see we packed just right; neither too much or too little. We brought the perfect amount to make our space feel like home. The familiar objects help ease the sense of in-between and dislocation.

We start to figure out island life. Our cars get new Hawaiian license plates. We walk the dogs down by the beach and discover new sandy places. We go to the farmer's market and eat a lot of salad and ahi poke and hang out by the fans when the heat gets to be too much. I get used to sweating in the humidity and delightedly notice my hair has grown a couple inches since we moved.

We explore the trails close to our house. Run by the sea, run on the red dirt, run the hilly Kauai Marathon. My husband starts to job hunt, and I start to put pieces together for creative projects turning my attention to art and children's books.

My parents move to the island in September, and in so doing manifest their move sooner than expected. Sometimes prayers are answered swiftly and grace descends into places we cannot see our way through. They found a few human angels in their realtor and local church who helped them pack, donate, consign, prepare, organize, clear, and get their house ready for the market, so they could permanently leave the state earlier than planned.

The day we pick them up from the airport I can feel the energy shift. Something feels different; it's a sense of relief and grounding and grace. I can tell Brent is happy we are all together, happy we are all here, and happy his ashes now reside in the place he loved the most.

Football season starts. I don my Patriots jersey in memory of Brent as we watch the games on Sunday while Dad makes a feast, and I think about what a different kind of late summer-early fall it is as the breeze sways the palms and rainbow plants outside the window.

I try new things and let my identity shift. I start going to hot barre class and learn to reconnect with my body in a way I haven't for a long time. I create a writer's page called *Island Songs*, and use it as a forum to share poetry and prose, giving myself a new space to grow. I learn just how serious Kauai's rain can be and find that tucking into my writing while the rain pours outside is its own form of creative cozy.

I realize as I write and try to share my new life that I'm cautious with how much of myself I'm willing to share. This new journey feels tender and precious and somewhat private. I feel the need to protect it, protect myself, and let the seeds of what I'm planting have time to take root and grow. I learn how sacred my space of self is, and I learn I now have very little tolerance for stress or drama or carrying anybody else's stuff but my own. Especially if it disrupts my hard earned space.

I start to root out the fears within that still hold me back. I'm scared of what people may think if I start writing about and talking about my brother. I'm scared of being judged. I wonder if people who knew me in my former life will think I've gone crazy.

I learn to work my way through these fears and simply respond to them with, "well so what if that happens, there are worse things." I begin to see the constrictive nature of my fears; they are limiting and reducing, and they are absolutely holding me back.

I get brave and publish my first article talking about my spiritual experiences with my brother. It is a huge milestone that requires so much courage, and yet my courage begins to pave the way for more writing as I realize on a deeper level that the sky won't fall if I talk about Brent. I can't control other's perceptions of that information. I can only ask Spirit to bring it to the right eyes and ears.

I make time to work with Spirit as much as I can. I make space for daily meditation and tapping in. I want to know the plan, and I'm not getting much of a blueprint other than a vague outline of teaching and writing and living the life that is immediately in front of me.

Sometimes I get this uncanny sense that Brent helped clear this space for me. That this time is meant to be a sacred pause so I don't dive into something new right away, busying up my schedule. Instead, he has given me the pristine gift of space—something I haven't had in years—leaving me with few responsibilities except to myself.

I go to the ocean. I hike in the jungle. I stop and take pictures of rainbows whenever they bless the sky. I laugh going down the highway when I realize there is a goat standing up in the back of the pick-up truck in front of me. I stop at fruit stands and revel in the delight of having time to drink a tropical fruit smoothie on a Tuesday morning.

I marvel at the fact that the back of my Durango holds beach towels, a yoga mat, and extra flip-flops; and I remember the days she held hiking shoes, blankets, and extra cold weather gear. Now instead of the mountains, we drive Beastie out onto beaches, lay down our towels, and hang out with the dogs watching the sun set by the ocean.

I eat fish tacos from food trucks. I nap. I write in bits and pieces. I let myself unravel and unwind. Life is simpler. I try not to obsess about when my savings will run out or *what next* or my bigger questions of what my future work will be. Sometimes I'm lonely. Sometimes I still feel dislocated and on the fringe. Sometimes I'm simply content and my soul is so brave and well.

Sometimes I just close my eyes and listen to the powerful workings and whispers of the wind. I bring her my questions, and she tells me what's more important than what I'll be is *who I be.*

Whistling and wailing: *Just be yourself, and all will be well, all will be well, all will be well.*

45

REIDENTIFICATION

I DENTITY CAN BE something both fixed and fluid. We are often called to grow beyond who we've previously been, and yet it is up to us whether or not we choose to answer that call. Oftentimes we have a feeling that something is out of sorts within us, and yet it can be difficult to give ourselves permission to follow that feeling through. We are tempted to try and press reset and make everything go back to the way it was, as sometimes following a feeling all the way to the end of a maze will take us to an outcome we didn't expect.

I find myself between worlds here in Kauai. My Alaskan identity no longer suits and hasn't for quite some time. Even while still in Alaska, I could feel myself straddling worlds; my physical body keeping time and finishing up my life there, even as my heart had traveled on ahead of me. Now that my physical body is fully planted over here, I find myself trying to step into a new identity. New faces, new places, new spaces. There is freedom in not knowing anybody here and not having anything set, even if at times it feels disorienting and lonely.

These aren't new feelings, as ever since Brent passed, I've felt a sense of separateness and loneliness from almost everything. Grief became a divide I found hard to build a bridge across. Now I find myself in this incredible, beautiful new space, and I am separate and alone in new ways. It's not necessarily a bad thing—there are gifts to having wide open space to find your way. But it leaves me once more not knowing how to feel and wading through new emotional terrain.

I realize I'm sifting through my pieces in this place. Trying to figure out what I still identify with and what I don't. What aspects of self I want to take forward and grow in Kauai, and what aspects of self I want to leave behind as part of who I was in Alaska. I feel the need to mentally distance myself from my old Alaskan life and memories, so I can be fully present here.

I realize that sometimes we toss all of the contents of our internal closet out onto the floor, so we can clearly see what was in there to help us sort through things and reorganize. I feel a sense of those contents strewn around the floor of my soul and psyche, as I go about the work of sorting. At times it feels incredibly confusing and messy, and I'm not quite sure where to start or what I'm even looking at.

So I do the things I know to do to bring myself back to me. Spend time out in nature and slowly begin to make friends with the land. Ground myself in love's power and try and look for the ways to bring love into my days. Remember that it's actually a beautiful thing not to know who and where you are, as it is only in that vulnerable, amorphous space that we can learn to take on a new shape; we can't really change our shape if we're entrenched in the boundaries of an old identity.

And in those moments of deepest unknowing, I try and practice patience. Reminding myself that this island has a timing all her own, life has a way of moving towards wellness, and the process of just living life will help sort the contents out. In the meantime, even if I don't know where I fit or where I belong on Kauai, I can always come back to a sacred space within and know:

I always belong to myself.

46

NEW STARS

I T IS SLOWLY dissolving. The residual layer of tired, loss, grief, fatigue, and heaviness that was pressing down upon me; I got so used to carrying it back in Anchorage, I had begun to think it was normal. I walked under the stars this morning and felt a bit more evaporate and dissipate beneath the illumination of night. Walks like this make me re-realize my existence—I am *here*, and here is Kauai, where life is thousands of miles away from what it once was.

How do we get so off track in our lives? We lay down roots and hope we laid them in the right place. Many times we do, at least at the start, but they don't always grow in the directions we want them to grow. And they don't always produce the kinds of fruits that help us feel nourished and satisfied.

I look at all my years in Alaska and remember my roots; many of them produced good growth. But in the end, all the new tendrils and sprigs and tributaries trying to shoot out had no room to go, and I felt that the gifts I have to offer, the most beautiful and tender pieces of me, were not particularly seen, affirmed, or valued.

And as human beings, we have a craving to be seen, affirmed, and valued by somebody other than just ourselves.

The land of Kauai breathes with a feminine energy that is in sharp contrast to the masculine energy running through Alaska's veins. There is sun and sea and a lightness in the atmosphere, as if we are on a different dimension that is one step closer to heaven. It is easier to hear Spirit, easier to listen to the elements, easier to nourish my intuitive gifts.

What I am finding in my nourishment is the gift of dissolution of the thick layers I was carrying, and the re-identification with what lies under those layers: a healer's heart who chose the road of Clinical Psychology as a means of helping people. A year ago, I just wanted to lay her to rest and be done with that chapter, but I find that I am not done—just ready to direct that energy through other means and write a new chapter.

Sometimes we need to actualize unseen parts of ourselves, help them feel seen, nourished, sustained and valued, if we are to integrate them into the whole of who we are and move towards greater fullness.

I had an unseen part that people caught glimpses of, but never really grasped the full, as if they were seeing me through a keyhole. People get so used to seeing you through a certain lens that you can change right before their very eyes, and they still see you as they always have. I kept trying to catch a glimpse of myself through their eyes and couldn't find what I was looking for, and it took the loss of a brother and the decision to make this major life transition in order to give myself a new mirror.

Here I am, finally finding what I need to see my full picture. I'm beyond grateful I've been given a place here on this island who is so alive with spiritual and natural gifts, that each day brings something new to help sustain and teach my hungry soul.

We can be no more than or no less than who we feel called to be in this world. It's just that sometimes we get so busy with the living that we look up and realize our life isn't growing in the direction we want. And when those times come, we find ourselves at the crossroads of change, where life sits inviting us to take a new path of the heart and grow beyond what we've previously known.

Sometimes it just takes a while to find what you need in order to take that path. But when you do, you will discover that despite the hardships in getting there, you wouldn't have it any other way. As you let life's new stars resolve, absolve, and guide you back home, dissolving all but what is most real in you.

47

NOMADS IN TIME

SOMETIMES OUR PATHS are lucent, we have a clear sense of purpose and vision about which way to go; circumstances line up to lead us there. Sometimes it's misty veiled where the fog obscures, but we still see the outline of shapes to help us navigate forward. And sometimes it feels like a pitch-black void where we're lost and directionless and must become like the mouse, sensing our way in the darkness, relying on other senses to guide us when vision fails.

It is in this black space that we stand to learn so many gems of wisdom on being human, allowing ourselves room to grow, and surrendering to the process of life. Because we all lose our way from time to time, it is part of the journey. We become like nomads wandering a deserted path, trying to figure out which way to next go, hoping that the obfuscation of the dark unknown will give way to the illuminating clarity of the light, so we can see our way once more.

But we are not always meant to see or know or have a concrete sense of what's waiting around the corner. It is only through the unknowing—of blindly feeling our way along the dark of the path—that we are forced to stretch and grow; to sense and trust; to bump into something and realize we're headed in the wrong direction; to learn to regroup and navigate by the wisdom of stars; to gain new soul experiences; to step outside of what is certain, so we can make space for the uncertain.

Any dreamer or risk taker or visionary who defied "No, you can't" with "Yes I will," anybody who is living life bravely, openly, and authentically by trying to follow the path of the heart will tell you: *It's not about the getting lost, it's about finding the courage to stay the path, to keep walking forward in faith—even when you can't see what's next. And trust that you are being led in the exact direction you need to go.*

48

HOPE STRIDES INVISIBLE

It is enough
to be still and soft
and gentle with
ourselves
for a while.

This human thing
can be achingly hard—
hearts break,
we make mistakes,
we punch our way through
thick layers of dark,
to try and find
our sight.

What's most important
is not when we fall,
or fail, but only
that we try to rise—

Hope strides invisible,
and it still guides these days,
helping us stand
and look towards
the light.

49

ANGEL

As September passes and October begins to unwind, fall comes to the island. Kauai's version of fall at least, where the humidity slowly lessens, the sun sets just a bit earlier, and the strawberry guavas begin to drop in spades. It's in this space of transition that I begin to notice something is changing inside of me.

It's a physical and energetic shift; my body begins to feel different. I have the distinct sense that it's humming. Strange sensations of feeling tingly and zippy and breathless often surround me. Sometimes I feel like there are feathers and wings at my back. Sometimes the feeling is so ungrounding that I have to go lay down. It's not unpleasant, but it's different than anything I've ever felt before.

I talk to my mentor and she says the medicine men call it "attunement." A process that happens as you become increasingly sensitive and calibrated to spiritual energies. I contemplate the word in my mind—*attunement*—and decide it fits perfectly, as I often have a sense of being a violin string. Tightened, tuned, plucked and played to get just the right resonance.

My every day ordinary is increasingly composed of the extraordinary. At times, I feel like a spiritual train station where energies are almost constantly coming or going. The trees talk to me. So does the wind. I can feel the ancestors of this island. Brent is closer than usual. The island speaks. So does the sea. Messages and channelings come to me daily, I fill up a giant notebook with what I'm receiving, most of it is messages on love.

I see pictures in my mind almost all the time unless I intentionally shut it down. I have an increased multidimensional expansion and awareness of so many mysteries and forces, and Kauai is plugged into almost all of them. I'm like a transit radio who keeps picking up on all the frequencies. It's dizzying sometimes, and I get the feeling that I'm supposed to learn to control my own frequency and learn to control what I tune into.

So I learn to ground myself in Love in bigger ways. I learn to be clear and say "not today" if I need to stay moored and anchored to this world instead of feeling pulled between worlds. I learn spiritual growth and also a measure of control—how to turn myself on and how to turn myself off. It's new territory over here, and I'm still finding my way in it, I realize there are vortexes here, and I begin to understand on a deeper level that people who are energetically sensitive—who *feel* energy—will feel differently here, and I come to a deeper understanding of my own change.

Just when I began to get used to all the strange zippy and tingly sensations, I begin to feel something else I have never felt before. I realize those sensations of shivers and bells and feathers are a presence, one I've begun to feel much of the time. I don't know what it is, though I can often feel it at my back. Sometimes it taps me and I jump; one time it goes whipping through the kitchen as I'm talking to my husband, and even he senses that the energy radically changed in the room.

It's a joyful presence. Beautiful and loving. I get a sense of delight and wonder that comes in those moments; it's hard to put it into words other than to say it stirs a melody inside of me I've never heard before. It feels peaceful, protective, gorgeous, and light.

After a few days of this, I am on a video call with a dear friend who has her own shamanic gifts. She is the only friend I have who understands the strangeness of this spiritual journey, as she is on her own parallel journey, and we have established a level of trust and openness for all parts of our life including our spiritual experiences.

As we're talking she says, "BethAnne I just saw a white light behind your back!" To which I say, "I know! There has been a presence with me for almost a week now, but I don't know what it is." To which she very sagely says, "Well, have you asked it what it is?" I begin to laugh at the obviousness of her statement. I haven't thought to ask, yet no sooner has that question left her mouth, forming a thought in my brain, when I am given an answer.

Angel. Angel. Angel. The word echoes over and over again in my mind. I have an angel with me. *I have an angel with me.* I have an ANGEL with me.

Of course I believe in angels. I have always believed that they are out there helping. Bringing a greater depth of peace to people, helping sort out the broken cracks in this world, helping guide without judgment so everybody can keep finding growth on their soul path. Sometimes I feel like I've perceived when they are close by, but sensing and *feeling* one in this incredibly specific and familiar way is something else entirely.

I try and learn my angel's name, but nothing clear comes through when I ask. I wonder if my angel is really Brent, and yet this feels different than when I sense Brent. I get the sense Brent may be close by at the same time, but this presence is another entity. I continue to ask the question of name, and a couple nights later I wake up in the middle of the night with a song running through my head from a grade school musical I haven't thought about since when I was in grade school. "Angels Aware" the play was called, as the lyrics, *Michael called a meeting, called a meeting, called a meeting,* sing and flow through my mind.

Michael, I say silently in the darkness. *Your name is Michael isn't it?* I can feel both the angelic presence and the assent. And just like when I first began hearing from Brent and I knew my life has just changed in a very extraordinary way, I feel I have this special, sacred secret once more. I'm walking around in a sea of magic, and I feel so aware and amazed by the mysteries. I clutch them into me and hold them with delight in my heart.

I learn that sometimes the presence is stronger than others, but for now Michael seems to be guiding me. I feel renewed encouragement and vision for my creative projects. I feel peace that passes understanding enter into me when normal life hits and stress rears its head. One time I feel both Brent and Michael at the same time; I have the odd notion they are telling me to write these experiences, teach people how one even begins to *see*. It resonates on a soul deep level; I am overwhelmed by the thought that I am going through all of this so I can share it with others.

And then an even deeper resonance occurs as I have a premonition that someday I will grow beyond just sensing and feeling and *see* with my physical eyes and not just my heart eyes. It feels like a blessing and a prophecy being given to me, and I weep in anticipation, hope, and the beauty of the moment. I wonder what will come to be even as I know for now, it is enough.

I've been on this island enough time to know things have a way of unfolding at their own pace. You can't rush these matters, and you can't force yourself to *see* before you are ready. And so I keep attuning and seeing with my heart-eyes and begin to get used to feeling an angel nearby.

50

RIBBONS

Rainbow weaves
orchestrate
a sea
I cannot quite see

Wrap their ribbons
around me;
sky breathes,
pulls me deep

Into the change
of mystery,
a world of things
unseen

Found only through
an open heart
and innocence
of belief

51

CELESTIAL SONGS

YOU THINK YOU can't make a difference, but just ask the golden flower or the song bird or dawn's new dew; and they will teach you of an existence where each note, leaf, and drop matter.

There is a universe inside every kindness, the earth opens up each time we love, and grace runs through the veins of these days telling us we each sing a purpose.

Faith isn't blind, neither is justice. *Neither is Love.* But each requires us to learn to see through new eyes, which can only be found in the heart, not the head.

If you look carefully, you will begin to see that angels are real and so is magic. So are the voices we hear on the wind and the things we see through soul's window.

We don't have to understand something to believe in its existence, this world is wrapped in mystery within mystery. Peeling each layer is how we find holy.

Somewhere in the seam where earth meets sky, the air whips with force unseen, celestial light sends shivers up spines, and within each breath a symphony rings:

I am love, You are love, We are love. All is love.

52

WRITE THE BOOK

I AM CONTINUALLY STRUCK by just how much courage it really takes to follow your truth.

I write these words 10½ weeks into our move to Kauai, under a starlit sky, as frogs chirp and other creatures of the night buzz and whirl outside my window. I haven't been writing much lately, sometimes, no matter how vital writing feels to heart source, you just have to tuck the keyboard away and experience the change before you are ready to put words to it.

It's a change that's been beautiful, but also very tender and confusing as I sort through my pieces. I keep pulling them out and rearranging them trying to make sense of my sequence. Trying to make sense of how one moment I was over there, in Alaska, and now *here in Kauai* I find myself, writing these words as I stare out at the stars that still grace a 5 a.m. sky.

Though I lived and experienced everything that got me from there to here, it's as if I'm integrating it on a deeper level. In a space inside of my heart and psyche that is making sense of it through new language and lens, as I continue to meet the unmet self I knew was waiting over here and allow her to coalesce, transform, and integrate into my core.

I haven't been able to see my full picture, but this week it started to come together and the next step on the "what next?" path felt so clear I wasn't sure why I didn't see it before, except to say that life has its own timing and we see things clearly only when our hearts are ready. This week my heart finally felt ready.

I realized those trickles of words that have been coming out—about my brother and all that has transpired since—are trying to tell me something. They are not just a blog post or a poem or an article. They are a book. The sequel to *Lamentations of the Sea;* the other side of the story.

I have all these untold stories that I've been carrying in my heart since the day Brent crossed over and they need to be shared. They've become a fire in me that needs to be released. This week I felt the task set before me with certainty, clarity, and fear: *You are trying to tell a bigger story here, you need to write this book.*

But I'm scared. I thought.

Write the book, write the book, write the book. The stars sing this song into my bones.

Am I ready to share these experiences. I wonder.

Write the book, write the book, write the book. The spirits swirl around me in support.

Can I really do this. I doubt myself.

Write the book, write the book, write the book. The trees lend gentle wisdom.

Who am I to say these things. I question.

Courage Little Sister—do you not yet realize that every time life handed you a close, you chose to open in love. You are a being of love, living in love, and you rest in Love's authority. Write the book.

Brent speaks it to me, and it is enough to help me gather up my pieces, find my brave and make a decision to begin to write these experiences. Besides, I feel so compelled by my heart and soul that I have a feeling that if I resist the message, that pull will only keep getting stronger and stronger.

Sometimes we don't come by courage easily. Sometimes courage grows within us as we set about a task and realize just how big and bold we can become along the way. I can't say I have 100% courage on this, but I have enough to keep moving forward, keep writing my truth, keeping doing BethAnne, and freeing my soul to grow along the way.

53

REMEMBER WHAT WAS BEST IN US

MY BROTHER IS with me strongly today. He sits with me in memories: mom's kitchen, rainy days, vanilla-icing thick on tender strawberry cake. Dad's suburban, an autumn drive through the twists and turns of the Turnagain Arm, "take me home country roads" plays and plays.

Remember what was best in us, he speaks to me.

For there you'll find joy and solace in your memories. I'm now in a space where the light shines bright—the dark of our worst is no place for your dreams.

Remember what was best in us, he speaks to me.

For when you feel love that is where you'll find me. Love is the key that will open the door so you can see I still walk beside thee. And love is the source from which we all came—it is life giving manna that feeds hungry souls. And love is the place I eternally dwell and the key to the grace of the truth of our home.

Remember what was best in us, he speaks to me.

Each kindness and laughter and each idle smile. For those are the moments we realize what's *real*, all else were just lessons for soul path revival. To wake us all up to the truth of ourselves and help us to grow into beings of light. We cannot choose love if the dark isn't felt, and we cannot choose hope if we don't know the night.

Remember what was best in us, he speaks to me.

For there in those thoughts, I'll always be. Here and there and everywhere, infinity's my galaxy. Far away, but close beside—no space too great to separate. Connected and bound from the other side—death is the door through eternity's gate.

I remember with him in my mind, a trip of joy around the stars. You cannot lose what you've already found—his essence lives on through the love in my heart.

54

OUT

WHEN I FIRST began to write about having an ongoing sense of my brother's presence in my life and all that transpired since, I felt like I was spiritually coming out of the closet. I felt vulnerable and exposed and like I was outing myself; sometimes I wanted to take the words back after I wrote them—I'd find my brave and then regret it later, the words felt too vulnerable, unsupported, and unshielded.

Through sharing my words online, I did get a few unfriends and unfollows, and initially that was hard, but it also made me process those experiences and realize you can't change the lens through which others see the world. *Or how they see you.* Either they are open to what you have to say or they are not. Besides, there are worse things than getting unfriended or unfollowed. Like unfriending and unfollowing parts of yourself, because you are uncomfortable and afraid of where they may lead.

When I came to Kauai I began to find myself feeling freer and freer to begin to share my truth through my writing and in my relationships. As time went on, I began to see that my connection to Brent had become such a deep and ongoing part of who I am, it would feel unnatural not to write about it. Like I was lying about my own being, and as somebody who embraces authenticity, I just wasn't okay with living a lie.

Sometimes it takes a while to be our true selves and show those pieces we most fear we will be judged for. We find our courage in small ways and big ways. Tiny moments and bold gestures, sometimes vacillating back and forth between brave and scared before we find the confidence to lay claim to something inside ourselves and transcend our fears.

We can't keep ourselves hidden just so somebody else doesn't feel uncomfortable—they are free to go their own way if they differ, so release them with love and grace to keep exploring their own life path, and then get about the business of owning yours. For we are the only ones who can know who we are on the inside, and we are the only ones who can learn to embody our truth and walk a path where our internal world is in alignment with our external world.

I eventually found that with each step and gesture, it became a relief and release and revolution to be honest and speak my truth. To step outside the weight of caring what others may think. To re-realize and remember an old truth that I keep living over and over in myriad ways: our truth of self is not for others to understand, it is for us to understand within our own heart and soul. And when it's pressing upon our hearts, we have to speak and share. The truth of our souls is what's at stake.

55

Divinity's Galaxy

These have been
the days of
time travel,
of leap frogging
over myself
times 5 – – – – –
then racing
to catch up, and slip
back into my skin.

I'm shape shifting
so fast:
this dawn
a bird of paradise,
this noon
a dolphin of peace,
tonight I'll reach
up and soar
to the moon,
we'll whisper of the things
that will come
to be.

Magic is
a golden interface
where imagination,
meets spirit,
meets love,
meets alchemy.

And these are the days
I am finding my way
through the heart
of divinity's
galaxy.

56

TRIBE

THE DAYS ARE getting a little shorter, and I've discovered that trade winds, rainstorms, a fierce ocean, and a later rise of the sun are what constitutes late autumn on Kauai. You wouldn't think it would get cold, but houses aren't heated, and it can become quite cool when a wet breeze gets going.

I find myself going inwards with the season, tucking into my studio for art and writing. I keep feeling like I am waiting for something to illuminate and shift, though I'm not quite sure what. It is an introspective space, a bit lonely, and I realize how disconnected I feel and have felt for a long time. I just don't seem to fully fit in anywhere, and at times, I find that painful.

I've always felt I straddled two worlds, like I was a part of things but not quite a part of things at all. Back in Anchorage, I seemed to move seamlessly between different groups and hubs that I belonged to, and yet there was still a piece of me that couldn't fully plug in. Those deep introvert, sensitive, spiritual swirls that make up my composition struggled to find safe harbor.

Sometimes I would come home when a social gathering had gone on too long or gotten too chaotic, and I would cry for no reason other than feeling overwhelmed with emotions, sensations, and an over stimulated nervous system. My inner empath and highly sensitive would feel so much all at once in these settings, and she'd need to release it through tears in order to press reset.

This invisible part of myself couldn't seem to connect, and my sense of that gap only grew larger and wider after Brent.

Now that I'm on the island, I'm hoping I'll start intersecting with people who also speak my language, because as much as I crave my solitude, I am also coming to see that I crave meaningful, spiritual connection. I crave spaces where I can talk about my experiences. I crave people who are on parallel journeys who I can trade ideas with, as we shine a light onto each other's path and grow stronger in our mutual understanding.

I crave a tribe, and I don't have one, and I've been looking for one for quite some time. It makes me wonder how many people are wandering about this world searching for their tribe; lost cords looking for a place to plug in, looking for the places they fit.

I expressed this sentiment to my husband the other night. Though our family is its own kind of tribe, a space of home, hearth, and belonging, I'm still seeking a spiritual community. I desire knowing people who value the books of information I can feel stacked up inside of me. People who have their own books to contribute in return.

I find myself trying to create places to share. I find I'm more open over here, so I've been writing about the more mystical side of myself, my experiences with Brent, my channeling, my sense of Spirit. Yet I sense it's not really understood or received, as if I still haven't found the right people who are interested in these things. *I feel like such a small drop in a big ocean, and I am lost in the many voices of the sea.*

Sifting through these feelings helps me realize that I am profoundly lonely with so much to share and nobody to share it with. At times there is a sense of urgency inside of me, like some sort of music is trying to come out, and I don't have the instrument to make it or play it. I'm not sure if I've ever been given a chance to play this kind of music.

I consider how a modern day Beethoven might have felt if he was placed in a soccer program instead of music when he was a kid. Maybe he'd even be good at soccer, and yet he still would feel something is missing inside, and he knows he has something in him that isn't been actualized on a soccer field. Maybe in school he finally gets himself enrolled in orchestra, but the only instrument available is the flute, and while making music on the flute is better than not making music at all, he finds himself staring longingly at that piano without even fully realizing why: *he is longing for a chance to play.*

That's how I feel most days—like I'm longing for a chance to play, and yet I can't even quite say what instrument I'm trying to play or what song I'm trying to make. I can just feel something in me trying to free itself so it has the space to form its melody. Hoping that at some point others may see the value in my notes instead of finding them odd or discordant. Or dismissing the music I'm trying to make.

It makes me think how we all have songs inside of us that get dismissed in this life. Good songs and bad songs. Beautiful songs and sad songs. Symphonies and lamentations and andantes and cantatas. And when we hear people singing notes similar to ours, we move in that direction and try to find others making like music, try to find a sense of tribe, connection, and a place to plug in.

Each of us hoping that others will find value in the notes we play.

57

THE GIFTS OF LONELINESS

IT'S LONELY NOT to belong. Not to fit a shape or tuck into a box or know where to find your tribe. Or to be part of a tribe that doesn't entirely fit you, so you always feel separate from the mix.

But maybe not belonging is actually an indicator of something else; maybe it means you are creating your own path, and you don't belong because nobody has walked this particular path before. Maybe not belonging means you aren't supposed to follow where others have tread but be the brave innovator who forges a new way and shines a light for others to follow.

Maybe loneliness can be a gift. A gift of void, creativity, and opportunity. After all, even Source was alone in its singular existence and out of that space came multiplication and combustion and creation and expression, so Love could be more fully imprinted in billions and billions of forms.

Maybe loneliness can be a blank slate or clean canvas or catalyst for creation that forces one to multiply and combust and create something new in their life to more fully express themselves. To express the love they have inside, which they are trying to uniquely imprint upon the world.

Maybe there is more to loneliness than meets the eye. Maybe loneliness is Creator's gift, and if we learn to harness and channel it, we can learn what it means to be creators ourselves. Innovators. Magic makers. Trailblazers. Visionaries. Dreamers. Artists.

Walking on the fringes in order to shift shape, so we can discover and navigate uncharted territory. Forever wandering outside of the lines, because lines were meant to be changed and somebody has to be the changer. Always pushing at the endless bounds of the universe, trying to fathom infinity's grace, so we can paint new pictures of love for the world to see.

58

BROKEN BIRDS

THERE ARE MANY of us who've been made to feel like broken birds. Somewhere along the way somebody—maybe a whole lot of somebodies—looked at us askance, judged us, said something cruel, did something cruel. And they failed to see us for who we really are, seeing a break or a bent in what was really a perfectly shaped wing.

They saw us as broken, not because we are broken, but because the lens with which they view the world is cracked. Except we usually don't know they've got a cracked lens, and so we internalize their perspective and from that moment forward begin to cringe and shrink, part of us perpetually bowed in shame, cradling our wing, as we try to heal and mend and make that "break" whole.

Trying to prove we are enough—not realizing that our own lens is slowly cracking the longer we see ourselves through their eyes.

Finding wholeness within ourselves is the realization that while we can't fix somebody else's lens, we can fix our own. We can learn to see ourselves through the eyes of the universe, who supports all life and who says we all have a place here. We can learn to see that our innate worth is in our very being, our very breath; not the things we do or who we know or how we look or who likes us; we wouldn't be HERE, children of this time and space, if we didn't already matter.

And we can learn to see how beautiful is the span of our own wings, when we find the courage to step into our own fullness and embody the only thing we were every truly called to embody—ourselves.

59

Sometimes healing and reconciliation with your self
starts with a single realization:
you were never damaged to begin with.

Not in your soul where it counts the most.

And once you can begin to wrap your mind around
your inherent state of wholeness, you can begin
to love yourself with fuller acceptance—
no matter where you find yourself.

60

RAINBOW CHILD

there are days
where the only thing
to do is return to a
childlike state of
wonder

take the gray dark
swirling about this
space; turn it into
soft raspberry mists
with daiquiri ice doves
curling upwards

cross crystal bridges
where gentleness waits
in better worlds
than the hard of
this place

yet there is beauty too,
pockets of kind, when
you let yourself unwind
in lemony sunder

see through the eyes
as the child who's wise;
who knows Love
is the rainbow that brings
the world color

61

MODERN MYSTIC

"We are born of love; Love is our Mother."—Rumi

I CREATED A NEW site: *Modern Mystic.* Maybe it will help me start to find my tribe. Or maybe you don't find your tribe all at once, and you just slowly learn how to beat the drums of your own song and trust that life will bring you the people who know your songs and are beating a similar beat.

It's a tiny thing—a little page on social media—but it's a new space, and I needed to make a space for this part of myself who is trying to actualize and wants to talk about Spirituality and Brent and Magic. And sometimes be a little mystical, even while being a fully grounded woman who will never shake her deep roots as a Clinical Psychologist, because I am learning—I don't need to.

The longer I am sitting with myself on this beautiful island, the more I am seeing I've needed to set that Clinical part aside for a time so other parts can grow. That side of me can be heavy. Part of that weight simply comes from overuse, and so I need some time to be lighter and be a different me. But the lens and perspectives on life gained through all my years of psychology will always serve and anchor me, and now I see in time that I can integrate and unify this part of myself with all the other pieces.

I also realize as I sit with myself that this is what integration looks like. A lot of times you don't know how your puzzle will look when it comes together and not knowing is terrifying and uncomfortable. *What will I be writing a year from now? Will I be teaching? Will I still be seeing clients? Will I be working with my intuitive gifts? How will these things come together? Who will I be?*

In the meantime, I let myself be lighter. I create my little Instagram space and have fun posting about the moon. I decide to start doing children's books and honor my inner rainbow child and artist. I keep seeing a few clients, noticing how life has siphoned many out who initially were still working with me when I first got here. In fact, many things begin to be sorted and siphoned, and I get the sense that more and more space is being cleared in my life, I'm just not sure for what.

I continue to grow spiritually, feel my angel tingles, and see Spirit in so many things. There are so many different energies and elements and forces and things unseen that compose the mysteries. Some of it I understand and some of it I don't pretend to; I am a student of Love, hanging out on the steps of Love's temple with the other lovers and seekers and mystics. Thoughtfully questioning, observing, and learning, trying to let revelation happen in its own time and its own way.

I begin to realize that I've been hoping somebody would come along and show me my way through all of this. Point me in the right direction. Direct me to my tribe. Discover me wandering and walk me home.

And in that realization, I also realize something else: just like nobody else could carry the pain of sibling loss and the pain of losing Brent for me, they also can't carry, own and claim my experience of personal transformation and spiritual growth. Learning about the unseen world, tapping into the energy of my brother, learning how these inner gifts work and manifest are things only I can do for myself.

I also began to realize that it is going to be up to me to create my own unique blend. That despite my yearning for somebody to reach in and see me and show me the path, so I feel connected and things feel easier, somebody doing that would rob me of the same ingredients required to actualize my gifts. *Self-knowledge, self-discovery, self-love, self-trust.*

I have circled back around to the familiar territory of realizing other people cannot tell you your truth, you have to discover it for yourself.

Our truths are for us to understand, for us to learn to live and breathe, and for us to actualize. While there are all sorts of resources, guides, and knowledge out there, which can help us make sense of our own internal experience, at the end of the day we are the only ones who can do the work of self and stand up and say—*Hey, this is who I need to be in this world!*

Sometimes the path has to be lonely, because it is the only way to fully claim and own your authentic sense of self. If it was handed to you too easily, if you had too many people holding your hand along the way, you would never develop the strength needed to embody and live it.

So here I am, dropping into this space of embodiment. Continuing to shed old parts of myself and old fears that get in the way of growth. Continuing to find courage to move forward in the direction I'm called, letting go of what others may think. Continuing to drop inside of myself and learn who and what and why I am.

Continuing to own my truth, claiming myself as a modern day mystic who is here to learn and teach about Love.

EASTERN LIGHT
Creative Integration

*Integration of self is a process, one we don't always
realize we're participating in until one day we look down
and see our puzzle pieces have rearranged themselves into a new pattern
in order to create a bigger, fuller picture.*

62

I Feel You in the Wind

I feel you in the wind,
the staccato of soft
mixed with crescendo
of cool, quick breeze;
you say you're still there and
you still love me.

I feel you in the wind,
the leaves wave in
a chorale of green, evidence
of this force unseen;
you've left, you're gone,
I carried on,
yet I still have so much grief.

So I give it back to
sky's whispered care,
who tells me you're here
on the wisps of new air—
that all beginnings
begin with an end;
that love lives on
when it's carried within:

I miss you my brother,
my family, my friend—
Now I feel you in the wind.

63

SIDEWAYS

SOMETIMES GRIEF HITS you sideways. You're looking ahead, not expecting it to come along, and then it runs right into you making you lose your balance. At times it's those moments that will knock you over hardest, as you weren't prepared to be swept into grief land and tumble into the missing ache.

But there are things you can learn in the tilted slant of this space, which forces you to shift perspective. Like how grief is almost always inconvenient, and yet it doesn't have to be unwelcome—it exists to help us process our pain and to help bring us back to a space of loving memory, so we remember what's most important in this life. Like how we think we know our own emotional terrain, yet can be completely surprised by what's sometimes buried in our own seas, until we lose ourselves in our mysteries and have to swim to greater depths of being.

Like how massively strong and courageous the griever is: for the griever is on a grief odyssey not of their own volition. They aren't allowed to get off the boat, and they have to find a way to keep on going and pressing forwards into uncharted terrain with only the stars and love to guide.

The sideways space is where you begin to learn your composition. The sideways space is where you face your hardest pain and find your way over, up, around, and through. *But most of all the sideways space is a potential invitation of opportunity.*

Opportunity to honor the love you have for those you've lost, kept in the most sacred place—inside your heart. Opportunity to honor and respect your own process of grief and growth and self. Opportunity to honor and deeply cherish the precious gift that is this life.

64

OUROBOROS

I CAN FEEL HIM behind me, sniffing, as I lean in to get mashed potatoes, gravy, and green bean casserole. I'm having Thanksgiving with my husband and my parents, and the spirit of my brother is present with us, as he often is on family occasions. It is both a comfort and a sadness, and a reminder that it will be two years in January since he's been gone, and my life broke from its old trajectory.

I have found that the ongoing nature of grief is latent. It can remain dormant, until something stirs it and you're reminded of how strong its presence still is. Like a part of your body that underwent surgery, something is altered inside and will forever be subject to aches, pains, and reminders of the wound. Even if time's passage begins to make it more faint.

Some days I deceive myself into thinking that I'm used to this new reality of normal. Some days I believe it's not deception, just acceptance of loss and the hard truth that I was never promised him forever—so I need to find gratitude for the time we did have. But other days there is a jolting and jarring sense that this is not how I envisioned my life: I was never meant to be the only child melting into bitter-soft songs of grief's sweet and gratitude's grace over holiday dinner.

My experience of grief often feels like an ouroboros eating its own tail—a cycle of wholeness where I can't tell where one thing ends and the next begins. At times I still hurt so badly, I feel I am crawling through the barren, wasteland of grief I was forced to cross the first 6 months. And yet it is because of losing Brent that I found myself at a fully awakened space in life where I had the courage to make profound changes to my life path and follow my soul calling.

Around and around these truths go, circling, chasing, completing one another. The same loss that ripped me to shreds being the very loss needed to force me to fully claim my life. *My brother's death wasn't just a doorway and rebirth for him; it was a doorway and rebirth for me.*

Brent comforts as he can. I feel his presence often. Sometimes he has things to say, sometimes he's silent. He's always loving. At times it's difficult to have him too near, his spiritual presence has become so illuminated with joy and light that it contradicts the spaces where the physical reality of his loss hits deep, and I need to sink into the darker waters of my human grief for a while.

I don't swim in those waters nearly as often as I did when it first happened, but I know my heart will always have the need to go there from time to time—revisiting, reviewing, remembering, reevaluating my own relationship to loss, love, and all that has come to pass since he passed.

Our world is a contradictory place where we often want to keep things as they are, yet are given lessons that ask us to learn to release and let go. Grief will teach you equal measures of both. Part of you will want to grab, grasp, and hold onto the past and the wish for a different timeline untouched by loss—*what would life have looked like had this not happened?* At the same time, you will be forced to move forward and do the work of acceptance, so you can grab onto the present day and build your life around the reality of what is.

Thanksgiving day I do both. Grab and release; reminisce and re-scind. We watch *Forest Gump*, and I use the poignancy of the storyline as a reason to let the tears floating behind my eyes stream full down. As I float like the feather in the closing scene, I reflect through a birds-eye view on the scenes of my own life that have already trans-pired, and the ones that are yet to come.

The longer I drop deep into my own relationship with grief, I keep learning that you cannot spiritually bypass grief. I still feel my brother, sense my brother, talk to the spirit of my brother, and yet the magic of those experiences does not negate the abject loss I have or the hole it left in the heart of my family. I can't use the information that he is now the embodiment of love, to wipe out the tender and true feelings of devastation a sister holds in the winter of her heart. But I can be comforted by it. I can let it be a candle and warm hug in the cold of grief. I can honor how his human loss and his spiritual revelation has changed me, and I can honor the journey of my own becoming.

I can keep doing the work of grief, which is simply to feel and acknowledge whatever comes up and know those experiences of loss are real and true and valid. For that is what it means to be whole in our humanity, and that is how we grow our hearts—by holding the ache and the light in the same space and realizing they come from the same thing. *I ache because I have loved, still love, will always love; heart's ouroboros of divinity.*

Some days that love asks me to soar to the skies and talk to the stars and see the glimpses of the mystery and miracle of the light of my brother's soul-life. Some days that love calls me to be a bridge and see the journey from soul to human to back again, and honor the path that we take. And other days it calls me to just be human. A woman, who feels more like a little girl missing her brother, sitting around the dinner table, remembering him.

Wishing he was there in person, instead feeling him lingering close by where he's smiling at the love in the room and the pleasing scent of mom's mashed potatoes.

65

CHRISTMAS LIGHTS

THE SUN IS rising farther to the east these days. The light is gentler in this season, December has come to the island and things feel quieter. I find myself falling into a rhythm and routine that is simple and subdued. I spend a lot of time working on my art, punctuated by trips to the ocean, trips to the trails, and lots of thoughtful walks outside to observe the beautiful interplay and light shifts in the soft dusks and dawns this time of year.

It's a contemplative space, and it suits me. So many thoughts and feelings are flying across my radar. The continued questions of myself and my soul path. A growing consternation that my husband still hasn't found employment, and the stress that is bringing to him and our household. Spurts of creative energy mixed with a deep sense of heaviness and fatigue. A childlike sense of excitement and wonder for the holiday season.

A deeper awareness of the grief that has come with the holiday season. I know grief isn't a linear process and that it can catch you off guard with its sudden presence and intensity, but even I am surprised by how much and how deep I am feeling.

There are now soft bittersweet tones of cool, gray blues woven through my life that didn't once exist. Those tones sing and cry water songs about fluidity, change, and the cycle of birth, death, and rebirth. They wash over and into everything I do, a tide of soft teals gently eroding the lines of my life, until everything becomes intertwined and connected. A profound sense of sorrow weaves through all.

It is in this space that grief's shrapnel emerges; fractured fragments that didn't get addressed or cleaned up or perhaps just weren't ready to surface when I did my initial grief work, and they decide to work their way out of my system now. One night I sob so uncontrollably and so unyielding, I flash back to the day Brent died.

I cried this hard then, it's the kind of wailing whose intensity and force makes you feel like your body will break.

I sob and I sob and I sob. Missing Brent. Wishing life was different. Realizing how much of myself I subverted when I was back in Alaska and the toll it took to continue my practice at the time. I cry because my parent's 49th wedding anniversary is coming up this month, and I am struck anew that I am the last one standing who can bear witness to the journey they've taken together. All the ups and the downs. All the change and growth. All the hard times and good times and times in-between: Brent was the only other witness to bear testimony to their journey, and now he's gone.

I have an unnamed longing for which there are no words.

I don't know any other way of being than to embrace my own experience of self, so I let these fresh waves of grief flow, and I try and take space to honor them. I listen to music that reminds me of him. I nap more, grateful I have the space to do so. I create my art and treasure my freedom. I try not to stress about the job situation and dwindling finances. I try and stay positive and keep my chin up, but sometimes it's hard—things are taking longer to manifest on this island than I thought.

And I put the Christmas tree up. It is a tiny Charlie Brown tree we found at the store, and though my murky emotions have me feeling a little resistant to it, I push through and set up the tree on a table by the window, smiling as I pull out the box of Christmas ornaments I packed all those months back. I remember what it was like to sort through and choose the ones that came with us, and even though life right now doesn't look quite as shiny as I envisioned at the time I packed them, *we are here*. And I am grateful, and I try and savor the moment of living what I dreamed.

Putting ornaments and lights on a little tree, preparing for our first Kauai Christmas. Finding the good in the moment. Finding the good in the day. Embracing the imperfections and bumps and unexpected emotional detours. Learning to take things as they come and let my feelings fly around my radar as much as they want, as they are all part of my palette and worthy of feeling.

Letting my cool blue tones wind themselves around the lights and brights and merry of the season. Not diminishing them or taking away from them, but simply taking their rightful place as a band of color that affirms how much I miss my brother and still ache from that loss. Even as they heighten my own sense of holiness for the gift of this life, wrapping themselves around the whole in sacred circles of love.

66

ESSENCE OF GRIEF

THIS IS THE essence of grief:

It is the loving and the missing and the reminders that hit sudden of all the ways your life has changed and all the opportunities you will not have with your loved one. It is the deepening and widening and stretching grief brings to your heart and the soul wisdom that comes from loss.

It is the ache and hole you carry inside that is uniquely shaped to who you've lost—nobody else can or ever will fill it. After a while, you learn to till the soil of that hole and plant roses of love in that space, so you always have a sacred place inside where you can kneel, talk to your loved one, and honor them.

Honor them and in so doing—honor you. Those who carry grief know things others do not.

What you feel is real. It is valid. It is complex. It is dynamic. It is achingly, shatteringly human. And it all exists because you have loved and lost. We grieve because we have loved, and we find healing and strength with that very same love. Love is our question and our answer and everything that lies between.

67

DIVINATION

Trying to divine
the nature of grief
is like trying to divine
the truest tones of navy blue
and deep, green
aquamarine.

Whose currents run
so widely deep,
their undertow
pulls
and tugs
and directs
the directions of
my streams.

My heart heals
in shades and lines—
straddling two worlds
of human and divine.

You're a rainbow now;
traveling
by my side,
helping me build bridges
out of pain and loss
and light.

My brother you are
one of the great loves
of my life,
I am broken in your stead—
And I am all the colors.

68

Holy Days

I FOUND A BIGGER brave this week. The idea flashed in my mind during barre class as I was staring out the window at the blue sky and drifting clouds, trying to fix my attention on something other than the ache in my legs from all the squatting and bending and tiring repetition. *Do something good for people this holy day season, offer something of yourself. Offer a free reading on social media, share your gifts, give of your heart in love.*

I was inspired by a friend who did something similar with oracle cards; her offering of a free mini-reading was such a blessing to me and emboldened me to pay it forward.

I have to sift through some dissuading mental chatter first. I'm a little shy about this part of myself, but even more so I am fearful of sharing this in such a public forum, and yet I feel so called to do something good and to put myself out there in a greater way. To take some of the confusion and grief I've been feeling from trying to find my place here, along with how hard the loss of Brent has hit me this holiday season, and transmute it.

Transcend the pain, transfigure it, do something out of love for somebody else.

And, quite truthfully, I'm tired of hiding. Tired of feeling like I can't share who I really am. Tired of being afraid of other's judgment. Tired of hiding away the most sensitive and precious pieces of me.

So I gather my courage, choose a day to share the post, and create the words in advance so they feel just right. When the time comes, I almost don't do it. I am surprised by what comes out in the moment—it is no longer the fear of being judged holding me back, it is the fear of failure. *What if people sign up and I can't deliver?* This is different than doing a reading in person with somebody I know—*What if I can't intuit from afar or for somebody I don't know well?*

Fear stays our hand, makes us small, keeps us in the current lines of self. Courage overrides fear, forcing us to try and be bigger, creating new lines. I have to remind myself that I did not come here to let fear hold me back then take a deep breath and press post.

Such a small thing, pressing post, and yet the journey to get to this space of personal offering in such a public way has been a strength journey of building new muscles as I climb new mountains. Of sloughing off old fears and values and judgments every time I ascend and descend. Of deep inner work of self-belief and intensity of purpose. My little post is both a culmination and a new beginning, and I go to a nearby mountain to go climb and ground and cry and just be with my own change: I would never have had the courage to do this 6 months ago, not even 3 months ago.

A personal revolution and evolution have slowly been taking place inside of me and this is a profoundly beautiful, big step.

In the end, 35 people sign up for readings. I'm teary, grateful, and a bit overwhelmed, but I try and have a little faith as I dive in. My fears turn out to be unfounded, and the feedback that begins to come in is positive, encouraging, and reinforcing. It helps me believe in myself a bit more. It helps me learn to trust Spirit in a greater way than I previously have, as I see that if I can just get out of the way of my fears and my self, Spirit will speak through. I start to establish a sense of reliance and competency that I haven't had the opportunity to establish before: *I can do this work, I am meant to be doing this work.*

It's a good feeling.

No two messages are the same, and I feel gifted in being able to receive the information, as it reinforces to me how profoundly loved we are and how Spirit seeks to support and guide us in all we do. I'm giving something of myself with an open heart. Something of Spirit. Setting aside old fears and trusting on a deeper level. Releasing old parts of my identity who are concerned with how people see me, embracing a new sense of self who is learning to depersonalize judgments and be herself.

One small step on the path, one giant leap forward for BethAnne.

A couple days before Christmas I sit on the beach in reflection, listening to Willie K's beautiful Hawaiian rendition of "Oh Holy Night." Reflecting on the beauty of this process and my gratitude for following my heart and offering the readings. Reflecting on the miracle of the season and all the sacred gifts it represents—love, hope, charity, generosity, humanity, divinity. I marvel at the journey that has taken me from Alaska to Kauai to this precise moment in the golden sand where an aquamarine ocean gleams against a warm December sun.

Brent meets me here and we hum together. *Truly He taught us to love one another//His law is love and His gospel is peace//Chains shall He break for the slave is our brother//And in His name all oppression shall cease//Sweet hymns of joy in grateful chorus raise we//Let all within us praise His holy name//Kristo ka Haku ho`onani a mau loa// Ka mana ka nani ho`olaha mau loa.*

Sometimes holiness is found in the most humble of moments.

Brent stays with me for a while. I feel so much love in him, in the notes of the music, in the blue of the surf, in the warm grains of tawny beach, and I give myself over to the oneness and let the holy wash over me, so grateful for the sacred gifts of this time and the sacred gift of my life. *I'm proud of you Little Sister. I'm really proud of you.*

69

GRACE PERIOD

G RACE DESCENDS ON our household for the holiday season. The matter of finding a job is still on our hearts but has been set aside until January, as we both realize nobody will be hiring at the end of December. My grief seems to have abated from the intensity I felt at the beginning of the month and that frees me up to embrace more joy.

Winter Solstice through the New Year is the time of year I believe in laying aside burdens, and instead simply being an activist for coziness, treats, and blankets. There is something about the pace of the days that lends itself to our own little island form of hygge where we walk the dogs prior to sunset and then tuck into cheese trays and cookies, watching movies while the rain falls outside and sky darkens.

We create a new island tradition on Christmas Eve and go to the beach at dusk to watch the light turn all shades of sorbet, then come home to watch *Muppets Christmas Carol* and make extra gooey cheddar mac and cheese. Empty bowls and full bellies and intermittent conversations about childhood traditions and favorite memories fill the space as Kermit sings in the background, and I smile at our eclectic tree and realize I like the night before Christmas even better than Christmas, as it's a dusk of its own.

The magical seam in the middle of anticipation and actuality, where sugarplums bear good tidings of joy and possibilities are infinite.

We fall into a strange time warp the week before the New Year, not quite knowing what day it is. It is a week that feels like a hello and a goodbye all at once, another sweet in-between of time, the jelly within two buttery halves of a biscuit, there to compliment and to savor. With raspberry laced naps and cherry candlelit glow and frosted raindrop reflections that lead to a quieting of the mind to prepare us for all that is to come in 2018.

Because making it to a New Year always equals 365 new chances for uncharted possibilities.

I find myself reflecting and writing down all that transpired in 2017 and my crystalline dreams and wishes for 2018. We share our intentions and hopes for the year, and I offer tobacco to the jungle trees in prayer, imagining those wishes pulled upwards on the silver tips of angel wings with tangerine lanterns of hope, so they may come to be.

It is a period of pause. Where new dreams, new intentions, and new beginnings are made, and even though I know that our better days are now— because life is a gift and so each day is a new possibility we can never get back—I still can't help but wonder what will be in the year to come and yearn for better.

And just like the season's Eves, I realize this is another kind of magical seam in the middle of anticipation and actuality where all that lays unformed in our hearts begin to take shape, where we create the steps of what will come to be in the dream space of golden hopes and carmine imaginings, and we give ourselves over to life's possibilities— both potter and clay—where desire, creativity and grace meet in the fold of the seam.

70

BETTER THINGS

I woke to the scent of palo santo
on the breeze, the faces of my
ancestors etched into my dreams.

We grieved together for all
that's been lost, and the clip of
this world's broken wings,
then turned our faces towards the sun
and dreamed of better things.

Dreams of hope and healing
where love prevails on hate,
dreams of illumination,
when reverence for life becomes
our sacred way.

Dreams of grace and tenderness
where shadows are washed and transformed
by the rain, dreams of new tomorrows—
where we see the divine in
humanity's veins.

Dreams of new tomorrows.
Where these days fall behind,
and we've reached for better things.

71

Change is hard.

Stepping into who we are even harder.

It requires a lot of brave risk taking, mistake making,

and learning to be okay with imperfections, not knowing,

experimentation, and a lot of leaps into the unknown.

But we are not meant for stagnancy,

we are meant for artistic evolution of self.

Our path continually being created with each brave new step.

72

Great Expectations

I T's difficult to relinquish expectations. We all have them, we all have a notion of what we'd like to see happen or how things should go. I arrived in Kauai with a boatload of expectations. I figured there would be a few months of an adjustment period, but then I expected things to fall into place. *I'm here on a soul calling, right? So shouldn't things magically just kind of line up?*

Yet that's not quite how things have gone. My husband is still out of work, Brent feels like he's gone silent, and I am still wandering around the fringes of the circle in search of my purpose and tribe. Some things have lined up, others haven't; there's been a lot of messy and challenging emotions that have come from that, and I'm learning that living a soul calling looks very different than expected.

It's hard not to expect. It's in our human nature to attach an expectation of outcome. Yet when we expect an outcome to look a certain way, we automatically give up some of our own power, agency, and peace by sending ourselves the message, "I can't be happy/content/okay/etc. unless x happens."

Placing expectations on Life is akin to getting into a power struggle with Life. Life will always win, and we can get fairly tossed about when we fight the current and demand things look a certain way. As I write these words, I'm reminded that I have already learned this lesson with the loss of my brother, and here it is again. Come round in new form:

We are not promised things will look a certain way, we are just promised today, because we are not here on our terms, we are here on Life's.

I begin to integrate and relearn this lesson in new ways as I step into the first few weeks of 2018. I realize I've placed conditions around my own sense of happiness in Kauai, conditions contingent on security, conditions contingent on stability, conditions that basically say—*I can't be happy until I know how it's all going to work out.*

Yet I don't know the how: I can't fast forward a year from now, peer at the future, and then travel back with the reassurance that things are going to be okay. Even if I could, maybe I wouldn't want to, as life has a tendency to take us on twists and turns we can't always imagine, sometimes we are better off not knowing what's waiting around the bend.

I am beginning to realize that this is what an adventure looks like. Staying open. Exploring. Going into uncharted territory, observing and learning the lay of the land. Falling down and discovering a side trail you wouldn't have seen had you not fallen. Allowing it to be what it is, instead of trying to shape it.

Releasing expectation and conditions and beginning to learn in a completely new way what it truly means to trust the process.

73

FLOW

THE PRINCIPLES OF allowance and receiving are on my heart as I write these words. Along with a thoughtful and tender contemplation regarding how I tend to be in the world—taking the reins of things, steering the chariot, and trying to make things happen in my life. What a beautiful gift when we discover our own agency and empower ourselves to change and actualization.

And yet, like any other gift, we get out of balance if we use it too much and just do the same thing over and over.

Seems like ever since I got to Kauai, I've been trying hard to make things happen and steer my ship. Sure, I give the universe a little room to do its work, but I get cranky when my expectation of timeline and the universe's timeline don't gel. So after a season of frustration, it's occurred to me that perhaps the universe isn't the problem, perhaps I am:

Maybe it would better support my process to give the universe a whole lot more space to bring good things my way instead of always trying to make good things happen.

A seasoned dancer knows there is an easy way and a hard way of doing things. Years of practice, of training your muscles and teaching your body to stay in alignment with itself, will produce effortless turns, leaps, and moves. Stop practicing or get something out of whack, and it's going to throw your balance off. And sometimes the harder you try and force it, the worse it gets.

Some things just need patience, relaxation, and breath—before you find your flow.

Our relationship with the universe is not so very different. The more we are in alignment with our self, our truth, our spirit, the more things tend to flow. The more we fight the process, get lazy and try to keep things the same, and don't give ourselves (or life) space to become whatever it needs to be—the harder, more arduous, and effort filled it is.

I learned from my dance teacher that you are never too good or too advanced to just show up and take class, no matter what the level. And I am finding this to be absolutely true with being a student of life and a student of the universe: *you are never too good to just show up and take class.*

So I'm taking class right now. Studying life. Remembering the lesson of how to embrace.

Remembering the lesson of how to let go. Practicing steps I thought I knew, but have been reminded—you're never too good to practice, train those muscles, and work on old and new skills alike, as your heart learns new levels of alignment.

There is a certain pattern and direction to things. Sometimes we have to trust in it, stay with its rhythm, and believe that when the time is right we'll find that effortless flow.

74

SUBMERGENCE

Unravelings happen
so we can knit ourselves
back into new shapes and hew.

Red yarn, yellow yarn,
blue yarn, gray yarn:
we change tone
and mood
and skin
as we shed the old
to embrace the new.

The soul has
a process all its own;
the heart a wisdom
only accessed through
sense and feel and color.
Obsidian lines mix
with calcite's light,
breakthrough found
through allowing ourselves
to sink and go under.

Diving the deep,
embracing our mysteries,
submergence becomes
our soul-bloods necessity,
we can't become more
if we cling to who
we used to be.

Knitting new seams
out of watery dreams;
the dark guides towards
new truth and clarity.
Rearranging our colors
into the person
we are meant to be.

75

THE WILD UNKNOWN

I T TAKES COURAGE to allow yourself to be vulnerable and sink into
your own space of change. To let the silk cocoon of the unknown
wrap around you for as long as you need, until it falls away and you see
your path with clarity. Most people fear this space and do what they
can to avoid it. They try and hit rewind, reboot, reset, and make things
return to the way they used to be. Even the body responds differently in
this space, as the nervous system searches for certainty and something
to anchor itself to; anxiety and fear are easy companions to find here.

I think of this space as the wild unknown and liken it to being
dropped off in a spiritual wilderness and being forced to find your
path, trusting your soul to help you navigate in the dark. Trusting that
the right supports will come along at the right time. Trusting that you
have been called here for a reason and that you will be given invisible
guides who help you along the way.

Trusting, trusting, trusting.

Some days you're in awe of the vast beauty surrounding you—
there is so much space for growth and room to stretch out and explore,
and you start to realize that learning to navigate by starlight is a gift.
Other days you realize how scary it is to feel so alone in uncharted
territory, and you work to calm the mental chatter that tells you to
turn back, realizing that there is no going back, there is only moving
forward. Most days though, you aren't quite sure how to feel, caught
somewhere between who you once were and who you are becoming,
and so you try and let your body and heart feel whatever they need
to feel and reassure yourself that although the soul process may feel
invisible, it is very real and you can trust it.

It is your own soul after all, remember that. You have not been
called to the wild unknown in vain, and you have universes within
that will help you find your way through. And so you trek across new
terrain, finding new ground and new gifts on the journey you didn't
realize existed until you arrived in that space. Trusting the divinity in

your soul knows exactly what it is doing, even if your human mind can't always see the full picture. Trusting your internal compass to lead you where you need to go. Trusting you are never alone, even when it feels like it.

Trusting, trusting, trusting.

76

STEPS

I WAS TOLD THIS would be a year of integration, and I feel that. Sometimes I look back on life in Alaska and how that life was no more the day we got on a plane and crossed the ocean to Kauai last July. I remember packing up the pieces of that life—those last few months were a cluster of stress and tears and anxiety and hope, and something I couldn't quite name.

I said goodbye to many people in person; others I just said goodbye to in dreams. I detached and let go of many things, some easier than others. Sold our beloved little cottage of rainbow cheer and coziness. Closed my private practice, which had anchored and sustained me for over a decade.

Shed an old skin of self.

Some days I still wake up in wonder that I'm here. Walk the dog under the stars and slivers of crescent moon sky, which slowly fades to gray to dusk to blue. Palm trees sway and clouds make art in the air, and the gentleness of this land overwhelms, even as it soothes me, and I ask the same question I ask every single day—"Why am I here, what next?"

Some days I feel the answer and my heart chakra opens in bursts of golds and pinks and purpose, and some days I just watch those palms sway.

It takes a while to reintegrate when we've deconstructed any massive piece that was holding our life together. I figure this kind of major life transition deconstructed where I lived and who I was, and it was very much needed, even though the reconstruction isn't always going as I planned.

That's the thing about life though, it has its own thoughts and ideas and plans, and they don't always match up to ours. And there is such space and vulnerability found when we learn to release our own expectation of how things should be and instead learn to trust in the unknown.

I'm learning to trust on deeper levels in Kauai. I thought I was already pretty good at that, but over here I am the student again, learning to say—

I trust I'll have what I need for this day.

I trust in my own process of self, which is slowly integrating who I was with who I am becoming.

I trust all will unfold exactly as it should, even though I have no notion as to how it will unfold.

I trust. I trust. I trust.

Easier said than done, and yet trust is where I find myself. Not knowing. Not able to see very far along the path. And having some sense that something in me is trying to expand and grow and change even more, and I need to make sure I am keeping my soil watered and nourished to allow it room.

The other day I was chatting with the instructor after my hot barre class—we've been sweating and burning and strengthening together for the last 6 months. One thing led to another, and we ended up on the topic that she has a group of women who wanted to do a woman's circle, but there was nobody who knew quite how to facilitate the circle.

I do, I said. *This is why I came here, this is part of what I want to do.*

And so we made a plan, and the circle will start next month, and I was left quietly reflecting on how life will show us the path when we put our intention out there, stay open, and give things space to happen. It's not the whole path, but that pink and gold and purpose in my heart is all fluttery—and I know it's a step along the way.

I trust. I trust. I trust.

77

RECEPTIVITY

These days I'm trying hard
not to try so hard.

To be in the blues
and the greens
and the yellows of the day—
let life's current unfold…
and lead me where
it may.

To reach when it's time
and rest when I need,
to live at a self-honoring pace
that acknowledges
the seas of
my introvert deep.

We weren't meant to be
in constant motion,
perpetually busy, busy bees,
but instead to take time
to experience life—

Be present in a moment
and simply receive.

78

MUD OR STARS

S PIRIT HAS ITS own timing for each of us. We sometimes want to be "there already" and somewhere other than where we are at. "Level up" without the work of going down into the tunnel of soul so we can dig for our truth and find the gems within.

The more you undergo this process, the more you realize there is no end when it comes to the soul, we are bottomless, and so there is always a deeper level to unravel; it is how we transcend our own prior gateways of self and expand our awareness into the infinite. We get tripped up, because we think we've already done the work. We've already dug to our deep. We've already squished around in our mud and come back with the golden lotus. Yet, that's often not how it works—there's always deeper truths we are invited to realize.

And so if you identify as a light worker, if you identify as a healer, if you identify as a sacred space holder, if you identify as somebody who is here to change the world for the better, then most likely you've had to dig. And dig. And keep digging. And every time life plunges you back into the mud, you wonder why you're there, you wonder if you're doing it wrong, you wonder if you missed the mark somehow.

Yet I would say you are right on target with your own soul growth. That anything falling apart is there so new space is created in your life. That it's possible that the new space may be even greater than what you've already imagined and is in perfect accordance with your own soul's higher plans for self.

Don't forget, we live on a planet of creative evolution. A planet who is always moving towards life and wellness, which means sometimes the planet itself has to purge and cleanse and dig and erupt in order to create space to align itself with new life. And since we've been given a place on this planet, we too are tied into its creative process and are each involved in a creative evolution of self, which moves us towards new space, new life, and new alignment.

Which means whether you find yourself in the mud or the stars, you can always trust you are moving in the direction of wellness. Always.

79

SUCH GREAT HEIGHTS

WINTER ON THE island may not be like winter in most places, but it's still its own form of winter. It rains more. It's windier. Cooler. The surf's higher, and the ocean crashes and roars with bigger symphony. The sun sets earlier in the evening and rises later in the morning, and summer feels a long way out. I find myself taking extra naps, moving slower, and daydreaming of magical places.

January has rolled into February and the household is feeling stretched, depressed, and directionless, as still no job for my husband has appeared, despite his diligent efforts. Getting a job has become his current job, and he has been at this for several months with nothing but a discouraging stream of "no's" and dead-end streets, as he comes face to face with the harsh reality of how difficult it can be to get your foot in the door on an island.

Finding a job has begun to feel like he's Ahab out on his ship searching for that white whale.

The more I stress and try not to stress, the less I seem to be getting done. And the less I get done, the more I am realizing that I seem to have little control over my own creative process. My projects stall out, I stall out, I'm not doing anything with my children's book or the sequel to *Lamentations*, which I was initially so enthusiastic about. If my husband is busy chasing the elusive Moby Dick, then I am sitting dead in the water feeling despondent and stuck.

I can't seem to force myself to do much. There was a time where I used to force productivity and creativity. I'd make myself punch through something, even if my brain and body were telling me to rest. I considered it a product of graduate school where my brain and body were often begging for rest, and yet the dictates of my coursework allowed little room for that kind of self-nourishment. I continued this pace with my practice and life in Alaska, and became used to running at a high-energy frenetic pace of always doing and always going.

Here life is slower, and I am trying to reverse old patterns and create new ones that better support my nervous system. I can't control when the job will happen, I can't control when inspiration hits and my creative juices flow. I definitely seem to have reached a point where I can't force myself—I learned this one day when I vowed to work on a few pages in my children's book and I fell asleep instead. And so I begin to work on controlling some of the variables I can control:

My relationship with time, my relationship with money, my relationship with Life, my relationship with Spirit, my relationship with self.

I try and look at time as a commodity and not a scarcity. Instead of focusing on the idea that time is money, and I seem to be wasting time and moving nowhere with my projects, I focus on telling myself I will have all the time I need and that everything will happen in its own time. I work on integrating the idea that if a project isn't flowing, it's because it's not the right time for it to flow.

I try and look at money as something renewable and replaceable that exists in abundance, even if I can't quite see that abundance. Instead of letting fear dictate my attitude, I tell myself that the universe will support me, and that new work will begin to appear and open up for me. I work on seeing money as a friend, "I will have all the resources I need," sometimes I am more successful than others.

I try and remember that Life is on my side, and that whether or not I choose to view Life as enemy or friend is entirely up to me. We are our own creators of the lens through which we choose to see the world. So I work on keeping my lens clear, owning my emotions and thoughts, so they don't own me, and finding gratitude for the day.

I try and remember Spirit is always with us, even if we don't always feel like it, and that Spirit will not withhold the good things meant for our soul path. I still feel my angel tingles, sometimes they are gentle, sometimes much stronger than others, and I begin to get a sense that there is more than one of them. I speak to them and ask for clarity to help me better understand, but outside of the faintest wisps of feathers and chimes, no deeper clarity comes through. It's frustrating, but I am finding these things cannot be forced, so I practice the art of patience.

Most of all, I work on my relationship with myself. I'm feeling in the dark, I'm feeling like I've lost my way. I'm feeling adrift and confused and wondering why I am here, like I've gotten off trail, and I'm searching for where I took a wrong turn and left the path. I'm not getting a lot of answers to my questions, and even Brent feels quiet and far away in this space.

And it's in this space of directionless silence that I really consider the magnitude of what I've done. There was a certainty to life in Alaska that I do not have here. Though I know that particular life had stopped suiting me, I miss bits and pieces of it. I miss security, certitude, and knowing how things are going to look.

The irony doesn't escape me; I left Alaska because it felt too old and familiar and too known. Not knowing is the whole reason I moved here. Not knowing is what I chose to sign up for. Not knowing is what I was craving in buckets. And I am finding out that not knowing, taking things as they come, and trusting in something you cannot see but believe is true—*is actually terrifying*.

I learn to sit with the terror and to become bigger than my fears. I refuse to let myself consider the possibility of failure. I feel like a woman walking across a narrow ledge, who chooses not to gaze at what lies below, because she knows she needs to keep going and doesn't want to freak herself out by looking down from such great heights.

So instead of focusing on what if I fall, I try and focus on what will happen when I succeed. I focus on cultivating my intentions and dreams. I focus on cultivating a deep sense of self-faith instead: *I believe in you, I believe in you, I believe in you. My dear brave girl, don't look down, trust your steps, and just keep going. You will not find what you're seeking behind you or below you—*

You'll only find your answers up and ahead.

80

HEART MEDICINE

Let the sky be your medicine
let the tree-speak brush away
a layer of tired haze,
there, on whiffs of cedar and sage.

Let the clouds help rearrange,
take from you and carry
whatever burdens that do weigh.

Let the pines and the breeze
and the winds and the seas
bring you back to the truth of the way—

You are seen, you are loved,
you are heard, you belong,
and my dear one, all will truly be okay.

81

Rain Days

G RAY DAYS ARE like blankets inviting me to turn in and delve within the hidden truths of my being. Thoughts churn and yearn; I feel the brush of angel wings, they've become familiar, as if it's simply a part of me.

Life is amorphous in this space. Unformed as the rain creates misty opportunities for reflection and grace. Where I tap into loss and re-realize just how much I've given up to become a lump of unmolded clay.

My intuitive-introvert heart seeks for a home and anchor in the gray. Sensitivity, sentience, and sensory reign. Imagination, intentions, and dreams weave in and out with slow illumination and interplay. Water wisdom knows that *grief is also love*, and helps me put shape to things that can be hard to explain.

Rain days are where I find my shades of nuanced self. They accord me the courage to stay with my mysteries, peer behind the mists and fogs of me, find a deeper awakening. Introversion becomes an art form as my heart curls into clemency, and I return to the truth that *love is the key*.

Raindrops give me permission to be. To let myself dissolve into my own beads of self until feelings are claimed and released. I hibernate in the rain. Let my seeds of self germinate. Give myself over to the unknowing. Surrender to the thought that I don't have to understand how things will be.

It is here in the blue I return to deep truth. Finding my real, re-forming anew. Let water remove old residue. Lending her wisdom to help see me through: *Love fiercely, walk kindly, and above all else be you.*

82

VIBRANCY

EVER GET AHEAD of yourself? Wanting to be something or some-where or somewhat other than what you are. Somebody else, someplace else. The future you instead of this version of you.

It can be hard to learn to occupy our present space, especially if we have dreams and hopes and goals we want to fulfill.

Sometimes we have a tendency to focus on where we are going instead of where we are at, and yet our present space is where the gifts are found. Not the future: we're not there yet, and it may end up looking entirely different anyways, nothing is promised or certain. And while the past holds gifts in the form of memories, they are fading gifts—like looking at a pressed prom corsage with tender nostalgia compared to smelling a vibrant rose bursting with life and bloom.

The vibrancy is *here* and *now*. Even on the days that don't feel particularly vibrant, there is almost always beauty to be found. Joy to be noticed. Love to cherish. Small moments of gratitude. Reflections on growth. Daydreams and imaginings that make you smile. Comfort rituals. The truth of breath. A new sky.

Sometimes you just have to stand still and claim the current space upon which you are standing and know it is perfectly, wonderfully, divinely, magically enough in this given moment. And so are you.

83

Don't Look Back

THESE DAYS, THESE days right now—they are our better days. I know it doesn't always feel like it. I know that betimes it's very difficult to find the good and to find the gifts. I know that, and I often live that difficulty, relieved to fall asleep at night and simply be done with the day when something's been particularly hard.

But I've wondered many times what my brother would have done differently had he known that we wouldn't be traveling into our 40th decade together and that he'd leave at 39. What might he have tasted more of. Enjoyed more of. Laughed at more. Appreciated more. Cared less about. Let go of easier. Found higher perspective on.

How might he have shaped his path differently?

I don't write that from the perspective that he has regrets about his life; in fact, every time I've sensed him in the afterlife he is nothing but joy and love and peace and content. No, I write those words for myself and anybody else who they resonate with, so that we are exhorted to remember to live without regret as much as we can while we are still here.

To live with appreciation. To take risks sooner rather than later if our heart is calling. To transcend our own mental chatter that says, *I can't,* and believe in something bigger than ourselves that says—*If your soul is telling you to go—then Yes. You can.* To embrace our own unfolding. To embrace our own unknowings. To embrace each jot and tiddle and line that composes the story of us, even if we don't quite know where that story is going.

Some days I want to be a thousand steps from where I am. On top of the mountain, instead of at the half-way point. I want to be more than the version of self I currently inhabit, as if I will somehow be better then. Then I have to take a step back, take a deep breath and remember—*our better is now.* Our better days are now. Each day a brand new possibility that can never be relived or reclaimed.

Sometimes I can feel my brother in those moments. He's so filled with radiant love that my humanness can barely conceive it; it's like trying to divine the true brightness of the sun by looking at a picture. But he's still so close and clear it is as if he's sitting right beside me, and I can hear him pure as a bell in my mind's eye—

You have to grab onto it Little Sister. Your life. Take it and run with it and go as far as you can. Remember the love, and don't look back.

84

FRESHMAN

F RESHMAN YEAR IS not easy. Since it's February, marking 8 months on the island, and most school years typically last 9 months, I've decided that I'm going to consider myself done with my freshman year at the end of March. April to June can be for the lighter lessons found in summer school before my Sophomore year starts in July when we'll have been here a year.

I call this freshman year, because in January I received an intuitive reading where some of the wisdom that came through was an encouragement to think about this time in life like being a freshman in high school. That just like in adolescence, where each year brings exponential emotional growth and development, I will have exponential soul and spiritual growth that will take place over the next 3–4 years.

That definitely wasn't the message I was hoping to hear. *Who wants to be told they're a freshman?* I've already been a first-year student 4 different times as I traveled the path from high school to college to graduate school to post-doc. Five times if you count the year following my divorce, which was a huge year of growth and soul stretch; I started over, a student of life and love in a new way.

But here I am, again, starting anew and finding myself in that uncomfortable yet beautiful space of unknowing, of building, of feeling a bit gangly and awkward and out of place as I navigate new hallways with new lessons. I look at the juniors and seniors who seem to feel so confident and self-assured, and I want to be one of them. I want to be somewhat and some other that I'm not.

I want to be plugged into the intuitive community and know what I'll be doing for my work. I'd like to be respected and seen and valued for my gifts, which I still feel are so hidden. I'd like to be able to go out to dinner without stressing about the cost, and be done with this college-kid budget that we've been shoe stringing along on since we got here.

I'd like my husband to have a job. I'd like the option of buying a house when the upstairs neighbors start their third load of laundry at 9 o'clock at night, and I want to stomp my feet in frustration over the dorm-room-like feeling I get when I realize I have no control over the noise in my living space.

I want a more fixed and stable sense of identity; this sense of constant change and fluidity that has been going on since Brent passed is tiring. Every time I think I'm getting a firm footing I find the sands shifting, and I have to find new stars to navigate by.

In essence, I want to be 3–4 years down the line; a cool junior or a prestigious senior. Yet here I am, only a freshman.

It is human nature to wonder who we'll become. It is a beautiful thing to set a vision for ourselves and seek growth and accomplishment of that vision. And yet when all we focus on is being "over there" instead of "here," we miss embodying life right NOW. Brent continues to be a reminder to try and live the moment and not regret, to remember tomorrow isn't promised and it may not look like you thought it would, so the only thing you can control is today.

With that in mind, I set about trying to find the gifts of being a freshman again. Trying to find the humble beauty in being only partially formed. Trying to find the gifts in growth spurts and awkward moments, which become profound teachers. Trying to find the growth in false starts and feeling disoriented and learning from those higher above me, remembering there is so much wisdom to be found and always new lessons to be learned.

One day among winter's breezy green and somber sun and rainy gray, I find myself walking the dogs along the country roads of our neighborhood trying to memorize the moment: *Remember this. You will never again move to the island of Kauai for the first time and have a first year here. You will never be this unformed again. You will never make another break at mid-life to follow the path of your soul. So remember this moment, remember how sacred it is. Remember the beauty of your own becoming.*

I begin trying to appreciate my moments as they come, and there are times a holy feeling settles over me during this season. As if I sense I'm passing through an invisible threshold of change, and I will come out the other side entirely different than when I first entered it back in

July. There are times I just feel February's stormy blues and try not to worry or be anxious about work and money and life, as I wonder how it's all going to come together and whether or not it will all work out. I am living my leap of faith; I just didn't expect it to feel so hard.

And there are times I find myself driving down the Kuhio Highway. Wind in my hair. Salt air coming in through the windows. I'll feel something alive and free open up even more inside of me, and I feel reassured in my bones I am supposed to be here. Not *over there*. Not *last year*. But *here* in this moment. Driving these roads, living my questions, finding my way through faith and heart-sight.

Learning to make peace with the nature of my own becoming.

85

Foot Prints

Live your life,
he said to me,
among the ocean breeze
of seaside songs
and fronds of palm
that wave in soft, wistful greens.

Pine if you must,
he said to me,
but please don't pine with length—
this life that you have
is yours to embrace
and I want your heart
to be free.

Weep if you will
he said to me,
but please don't weep too bitterly—
for your ocean songs
hold joy as well,
and you were meant
to sing of the beauty.

Live your life,
he said to me,
grief may be a necessity—
but so is love
and light
and grace,
and your soul has
the right to be happy.

What should I do?
I'm lost without you,
I said to the clouds
and the sky and the trees.

Then there he was
keeping time with the sea,
the sun shining down
mitigating my grief,
a presence of love
on the gold of our beach,
and this is what
he told me—

You're never alone,
I still walk beside thee.
So carry on Little Sister.
And live your life.

86

SOUL CALLINGS

S OUL CALLINGS CAN be messy, let me be clear. Answering a calling of the soul is likely to pluck you out of one life to place you in another. It is likely you will be forced to make a break from who you once were in order to become who you need to be.

Not everybody is going to go with you on this journey—in fact, there will be many you leave behind, and that will be painful. But many only see things through a one-dimensional lens, and so they don't understand your deeper journey or your deeper path; in fact, they may reject the journey and mock the path.

Soul callings will leave you wandering in the wilderness. Going through many dark nights of the soul. Things will not be neat or square and certainly not linear. Mistakes will be made, failures will happen, messes frequent; illumination and resolution and direction can be a long time coming.

But despite all of this, despite all the doubts and confusions and "where is this going" and questions of your own sanity—you will feel compelled by something inside of you. You will feel drawn to the light and drawn to the mysteries. Drawn into a deeper relationship with the universe itself. Drawn into a deeper relationship with Love.

You will seek more and crave more and find you are not satisfied with one-dimensional reality; that in fact you are seeking a multidimensional life of creativity, connection, and relationship. Seeking deeper truth and knowledge and wisdom that can only be gained through living it. Seeking to serve and heal and shine and be a transcendent light.

And that is why you have to pass through so much darkness. Those who shine the brightest didn't get that way from living life "right" and being "good," or being perfect and having everything add up on paper. Those that shine the brightest have usually walked through fires so strong they burned away all that wasn't real. They have descended into internal hells so dark, they didn't believe they'd find their way out.

They have fallen into abysses and grand canyons of soul pain so deep they scarce knew how to traverse and ascend the terrain.

They have made hard choices. They have made leaps of faith. They have been asked to trust when they couldn't see the way. They have been asked to bring love and healing into spaces that didn't look very lovable or healable. They have been purified. Sanctified. Set aside. They have been stretched, broken, grown, shifted, transmuted, transformed, and transfigured throughout the course of their experiences.

And they are the ones—from all backgrounds, all creeds, all colors, all beliefs—who have been called to be the healers and light-workers and game-changers and compassion-makers and consciousness-awakeners and way-showers of this world.

They are the ones who have been called to the cause of LOVE. And so as difficult as it may be—they know they can trust their path, and they know they *have* to trust their path. Because what has been touched by LOVE and blessed by LOVE and claimed by LOVE and guided by LOVE—can never be lost and never be ripped asunder.

87

PEACE SONG

This world is not
for the faint of the heart,
for there are things
that will make your heart
faint and hurt and break.

And yet those of us
with tissue paper skin,
keep finding ways to
let light in and fold
our breaks
into origami cranes
of hope and beauty:

Sunstone stargazers
who know there is
more than this veil,
that Peace beats beneath
an unknowing earth.

Softly it sings
with prayer-tipped wings—
Love will be our sanctuary.

88

MAKING BROKEN THINGS WHOLE

Break a vase, and the love that reassembles the fragments is stronger than that love which took its symmetry for granted when it was whole.
—DEREK WALCOTT

THIS PAST SEASON has put an increasing strain on the vase of my marriage. Hardship puts pressure on its sides. Cracks widen, water leaks, pieces start chipping and falling. I wonder if we're going to be able to hold it together. Finances. Identity. Disappointment. Relocation. Rejection. Stress. Adjustment. The on-going job hunt. *What will be, what will be, what will be:* I am not the only one searching for who I am, wandering along the fringe of the wilderness, looking for my place on this island.

Though beautiful, china is fragile. Though transparent, glass can easily break. Though elegant, porcelain chips. *I am left with the question of what are we really made of.*

Love is a choice. One we make over and over again. One we choose to make within ourselves and one we choose to make with those we love. Betimes we don't see how to make it and have to find our way through the murky mud of doubt, anger, bitterness, resentment and confusion in order to find the love in a situation, forgetting that the humble lotus growing in the mud offers a message of hope and beauty that something exquisite can come from something dark.

It is in this muddy space that I begin to realize our roots—*he is still here and so am I.* Two lumps of clay being remolded by this island. Still side by side, even if our vase will eventually look different than it once did—the foundation still remains. And that says something.

Sometimes love is gritty. It has to be if it's going to remain. It is in this gritty space that love begins to take deeper roots. It is in this space that the ugly feelings that have accumulated have permission to come to the surface so they can be transmuted, released, and healed. It is in this space we are forced to grow bigger and transcend the shape of who we once were.

We are still both in this together. We are still both here together. Friends to the end, so let's mean it.

Bicycles and pups and chips and salsa abound that particular day. A celebration of a slate cleared and a renewed commitment of togetherness. This is love and it can be messy and muddy but it is real, and it is us, and we choose it despite circumstances. We choose it without a guarantee things will get better or that my husband will get a job. We choose it without knowing what our lives will become here and who each of us is becoming.

We choose to rebuild the vase, because we believe in the inherent value of that vase and that it will become even stronger than it was before.

One week later a call comes from the Grand Hyatt for an interview. Three weeks later a job offer comes through. It's a shift and a hope and a relief, and it is needed. And I am so grateful. But I don't forget that we chose love before any of that transpired.

Taking our pieces, rebuilding, repairing, transcending, believing, loving. Turns out we are a kintsugi vase who glued itself back together with liquid gold—Love. Becoming more beautiful than we were before. Taking something broken and making it whole.

89

Trusting the process is hard,

I had no idea how hard it was going to be.

Yet the more I sink into it and surrender myself into

a greater space of unknowing, the more I am finding

that it's a beautiful dance to live a life

where you don't have to know what's waiting

around the bend until you actually get there.

90

SOUL LESSONS

W E'VE NOW BEEN here 9 months. I have visceral feels and a felt-sense of this time last year as this was the beginning of the end of life in Alaska, and March through June were about to become mad months of goodbyes, letting gos, and taking care of the tangible steps needed to move. I tire even thinking of it now.

At the time, I had an unmet self I knew was waiting in Kauai along with a great curiosity for who I would become there. Now that I'm here, I'm finding the answers to my questions through the process of simply experiencing the change and continuing to give myself room to morph.

Identity is a funny thing; both fixed and fluid. We attach certain ideas to who we think we should be, even as each of strives towards growth and change. And growth, being what it is, has a way of occurring differently than we expected it to look.

I came to this island with a sense of who I was going to become over here, and I feel like it's all moving in the right direction, but it's happening at a different pace and in different ways than I expected. And I have learned in a deeper, very humbling way that Spirit works at its own pace, soul callings have their own way of unfolding, and when you go against your own flow you only end up feeling thwarted and frustrated.

Whatever I expected to step into over here is still a ways away, which doesn't mean I haven't still stepped exactly where I need. It can take a while to shed the pieces of an old identity, even longer to integrate and allow life to bring you the new pieces that you need.

All in all, 9 months isn't that long and in my impatient humanness, I wanted to run before I could crawl. Kauai is teaching me patience, and the gifts of a good crawl, which will keep you closer to the earth, remind you how dependent you are on the ground that holds you up, and bring you to a space of humility, as you realize you were never really in charge to begin with. Life is in charge. And it's okay to let it call the shots.

In contrast to this time last spring where I had to grab my life by the reigns and manifest a move in order to leave Alaska, this is a different space. One of surrender. One of receptivity. One of crawling and noticing the gifts. One of allowing whatever will be to be.

91

Transformations of The Sun

A SHIFT IS IN the air. Almost April. My husband has started
working. After a season of confusion, disillusion and further
dissolution—I've come back round to myself after realizing I wasn't
truly living in the *now*. That happiness isn't going to somehow
magically be found one year from now, happiness is happening right
now. It's just up to me to find it.

Something shifted the day I fully tapped into that, when I realized
I wanted to be shinier and bigger and more advanced than where I
am at. So much further along my soul path. And yet this is where I'm
at. I'm not on the mountaintop, I'm halfway up, which doesn't mean
there isn't still a view.

I made an intention list that day which had whimsical goals like: "I
want to be creative and happy. I want to write poetry about crystals and
love and the moon and things of that nature. I want to embrace change,
all while appreciating the gifts of right now. I want to keep my heart
open, and never forget that everything has its own wisdom to offer."

The list brought me back to myself, and drove a stake in the sand
that said, *I want to embrace and cherish who I am now.* Sometimes
keeping our heart open simply means keeping it open to our own self.
Keeping it open to our moments and moods and beautiful humanness.
*Even when we're not exactly where we want to be, which doesn't mean it
isn't exactly where we need to be for our own soul growth.*

And with that thought, a new book began to birth itself. I didn't
even know I had it in me, except it is *all me*. I've been trying to work
on a follow-up to my grief book *Lamentations of The Sea*, with a focus
on my interactions with my brother in the spirit world. At first, I felt
so strongly Brent had things to say and wanted me to write this book
for both of us, but nothing has come through for months.

I have been a writer who isn't really writing, and then I had a mo-
ment of epiphany. *Why not write about right now? Why not write about
life and these changes and leaving Alaska for Kauai?* Instead of busting out

some book on the afterlife, which I'm clearly not fully ready to write, why not write an in-between book that builds a bridge and tells the story of who I became after loss and how the loss of Brent fundamentally changed me, grew me, and forced a new beginning and becoming?

It occurs to me that I was trying to go from *Star Wars* to *Return of The Jedi* without telling the transitional story of *The Empire Strikes Back*. Without telling the story of how Luke became a Jedi, or got lost in the dark of the degobah system, or battled his confusion and terror when he couldn't clearly see his way along the path.

The other book I was trying to work on is parallel to the lessons I've had this last season in life: I'm trying to be ahead of where I'm at. It's not time to write it yet. I'm not a Jedi. I'm in training and I'm still finding myself and trying to see the path. But that doesn't mean there isn't still something of value to write.

Start with right now. Start with where you are at. Love yourself where you are, and tell this story. At times we just don't see what's right in front of us, and then something happens that shifts our perspective and we wonder how we missed the obvious.

So I decided to write the story of life right now, and this story is ready to be told, because after sitting with writer's block for months I am now barely keeping up with my own words. But I guess that is just the way creativity flows. Creation really is a strange phenomenon, one minute non-existent, the next minute ready to birth itself making you realize that it was never non-existent: you were just in gestation and you didn't know it.

I realize this book has actually been writing itself for a while. Through poems and posts and blog entries and journal entries. Bits and pieces of who I am, as I searched for the meaning and truth of my own change. I realize Brent might still have more to his story to share, but I can feel a resonance in the deepest part of my cells, which says—tell your story first.

Tell your own story of transition, transformation, and change.

There are moments when I am writing that I can feel Brent nearby, the sense of approval and applause is so encompassing I dissolve into tears. I now understand and know that he didn't go silent on me this last season, he was just giving me space to be me, knowing I would take that space, go dive for my pearls, and find new growth.

Help me write this, I said.

No Little Sister, you don't need my help. This is your story, your book, and it's already all within you. But you do have my support. Always.

His words are a benediction and my flow continues as stories I didn't know I had stored up inside of me begin to pour out. Stories about grief and how it changed me, stories about Brent and what that first felt like, stories of feeling alienated and isolated and searching for my tribe. Stories of love and sadness; beauty and pain. Everything in me vibrates with the rightness of these stories.

It is my truth. And writing it allows me to creatively integrate on a deeper level than I have before. Realizing everything has unfolded exactly as it should. Realizing all the questions and fragments of identity have been an invitation to step into a bigger, more fuller version of myself.

One who now lives under the light of Kauai's sun; letting its medicine go about the work of continuing to transform and render change.

INTO THE WEST
Finding BethAnne

*The bravest thing you will ever do in your life
is give yourself permission to meet and then become
the person you are meant
to be.*

92

SACRED CIRCLES

T HERE ARE CERTAIN truths in our lives that we will keep spiraling around to again and again.

Like a constant reawakening where the shells fall from our eyes and we suddenly see more clearly, we will continue to lose our shells from time to time as we arrive at deeper levels and meanings of our truth. Our work is never done, self-discovery our life's work.

We have a tendency to think we should be finished with something. Learn the lesson, have an insight, be "over" it; but the truth they don't tell you is that life isn't about being over anything, life is about learning to be all things. Embracing all experiences, all aspects of self, all shades of our full.

And so we form sacred circles back round ourselves. Sometimes wounds we thought were healed, old memories we believed laid to rest, and past pains we thought retired get re-churned up, and we wonder why they've come knocking again.

They've come knocking again so we can keep learning. Keep meeting unrealized aspects of self. Keep realizing and actualizing who we are. Keep releasing old wounds, old thought patterns, and old ways of being on deeper and deeper levels.

Until one day we will have spiraled so deep into the truth of our core that we will see that it all comes back to love, every moment and each lesson an opportunity to learn love is the force that's been drawing us inward all along. Because to discover the self is an act of love. To know yourself down to your deepest level is an act of love.

To honor your truth and find the courage to live it? Is the essence of what it means to fully embody self-love.

93

GOLDEN SOLITUDE

THE NATURE OF the intuitive-introvert heart is a yearning for introspection, quiet daydreams, imagination, and acres of amorphous space. It may look like I'm just staring out the window to others, but really the first notes of a symphony are beginning to play in the drift of the clouds, as the trees speak poetry, and the chickens tell silly jokes, while the plants whisper insights of earth wisdom.

Intuitive-introverts find things in these spaces of uninterrupted quiet that they cannot find anywhere else, which nourish the deepest needs of soul. This space is our oxygen, and when it goes unmet, we will start to feel the lack and find ourselves gasping for air. If we gasp long enough we may even get used to surviving on low oxygen rates, but we'll never thrive. An over-structured schedule, interactions with others, going out in public, too much environmental simulation, having to step into a role or fit a mold are the antithesis of this space—and so too much time engaging in these tasks creates a solitude wound.

What a challenge to live in an overly busy world that devalues silence and this particular way of being, which doesn't come across as very productive or resourceful or practical. And yet the seeds of creation are nurtured in this space. Ideas are born. The spirit and mind travel to other worlds and bring back new discoveries to share in this world. This is the place where the seekers and artists and dreamers and mystics gather, creating light and beauty and love on a planet often fraught with gray.

The only way the intuitive-introvert can make space for such spaces is by healing the solitude wound. By learning to honor the heart's deep need for it. By learning to realize that saying *yes* to this particular part of your soul is more important than saying *yes* to almost anything else and the only place you'll find your highest truth. By learning to paradigm shift, run counter-clockwise and counter culture, and seek after what too few seem to cherish or seek—

The sacred world of the in-between, which can only be found through golden solitude.

94

INTO THE CURL

She craves quiet like blankets.
Soft spaces of nothing to tuck into and create.

Sunsets and crystals and fairy rings that pull her
up into the mysteries.
Imagination and space to listen and perceive.

She seeks the veil of in-between
to better see within worlds.
Moonlight and mermaids,
star streams and sunshine's rhapsody;
it's here in these spaces she leans in and curls.

Dreaming, seeking, following her
heart speak and soul wings.
Flying to her deeps and finding her pearls.

95

MAGICIANS

WHAT PEOPLE OFTEN don't know about the highly sensitive, the intuitive, the empath, the creative, the healer, the psychic, the energy sensor, the heart that feels/sees/hears/perceives to the deep— is that they don't fit the paradigms and boxes most commonly found in this world.

Most of us will learn to make a good show of "fitting in," but it's not the real self, it's simply an adaptive, lesser version of self that was developed as a survival skill, because the alternative of feeling isolated, rejected, and alienated is too painful.

So you learn to tuck away the most beautiful parts of you from a young age the moment you hear some version of "you are too sensitive, you need to grow a thicker skin to make it in this world." Growing up becomes a lesson on suffocation and learning to fold yourself into pretzel twists to fit the molds society expects of you; soul growth becomes a lesson on learning to unfold and stretch those limbs and reject old molds that do not fit, as you empower yourself to create your own.

You will think these abilities are a curse until you learn to see them for the gifts that they are. After all, not everybody sees and feels in color or can tell that who somebody says they are may be completely different from the energy emanating off of them. Not everybody can hear tree speak or journey in their dreams or listen to wind's voice.

And not everybody can love so hard you break your own heart and have to keep reforming it anew until your heart gets so big it holds the stars—and you realize your heart was never truly broken, it was just being stretched wider and vaster, until it grew so spacious it became capable of grasping love's infinity.

Nobody will tell you these things are gifts as you're growing up. They may not even tell you as an adult. You might be one of the ones out on the cusp, feeling alone, as you wander far outside the lines drawn by others, finding your wisest friends are sky and sun and sea.

But I will tell you it is a gift. I will tell you your gifts are magic; you, a Magician, with love being the greatest magic of all. I will tell you that your way of being in the world is valid, and it is not you who needs to change to better suit this world, it is your world you need to change to better suit you.

I will tell you that sensitivity, creativity, compassion, and love are exactly what we need to bring heart wisdom back into this place. I will tell you to never settle for a box over the freedom of your wings. And most of all, I will tell you—there is nothing wrong with you, you are beautiful, you are perfectly imperfectly you. And you are valued, needed, and seen.

96

NEW SEASON

THE SUN IS rising eastwards again and setting further into the west. It's April on the island, and I'm finding that I like the gentle shifts that signal Kauai in the spring. Flowers that slumbered throughout the winter months are opening up. The gray hues of the ocean that marked the passage of the new year are giving way to brighter turquoise and aquamarines.

And I've been reflecting on the passage of time and how the seasons mark our own times and seasons in life.

Integration is an interesting process. One you need to experience and live before you can fully write or talk about. I've been working on *Transformations of The Sun*, which is giving me a wider scope and deeper look at who I've become since losing Brent. The book is becoming both a microscope and a telescope, which is giving me new angles and perspectives.

Piecing together the manuscript has helped me piece myself together in deeper ways. It's like every day we are given experiences that provide us with a new puzzle piece to the bigger picture of who we are. Sometimes we need space and time so we can more fully assemble the pieces and understand what we are looking at.

Last year I was disassembling all the old pieces of my Alaskan life, this year I am slowly putting new pieces together of who I'm becoming in Kauai. I still can't see the full picture, but one thing is for certain: *there is an incredible difference between contemplating a change and actually living a change.*

I've had to learn to live a deeper life of trust on Kauai. Trusting the process. Trusting life to make a way. Trusting I'll be supported in this faith leap.

Trusting there is a season for everything. It occurs to me that the lavender sunrise, the thousands of songbirds, and the gentle pink bromeliads, which greeted me on my morning walk are not worrying about tomorrow, and they are definitely not worrying about how things will look this summer. Instead, they are just doing their thing—shining and singing and blooming—right now.

We can learn a lot from nature when we stop and pay attention, and I am reminded that my questions of—*What happens next? What am I doing over here?*—have already been answered by nature's wisdom.

Do not worry about tomorrow—just shine and sing and bloom right now, and keep trusting life to make a way when it is time for a new season.

The jungle outside my window is brilliant in her emerald visage; she sounds like she's speaking extra loud and joyful this morning. I have a clean slate of a day with nothing to do but write, create, and work on my projects. Trusting all will unfold as it should; putting together the pieces of me under the jungle's laughing gaze.

97

THE WOUNDED HEALER

"To be at home in the darkness of suffering and there to find germs of light and recovery with which, as though by enchantment, bring forth the sunlike healer." —KERENYI

As April moves along, I feel a shift is coming, and I feel it has to do with new opportunities for healing work. The answer to my "what next" question feels a little closer. Though it feels just around the corner, perhaps 2 or 3 months out, it also feels like I still have some work to do on myself before it will manifest.

I came to Kauai to heal something inside me, even though I wasn't entirely sure what. I believe back in Alaska I was seeing pieces and fragments of what that might be. An unmet self. A woman burned out on always caregiving. A sister who didn't have the space to fully grieve. An intuitive whose gifts weren't being fully utilized or seen.

Those pieces started to emerge during my time on the island. New aspects of self began to slowly rise up and stretch and take their space. Transitioning from a full-time practice to a small tele-health practice has been a thing of beauty; I stopped feeling like an accordion who was constantly being smooshed together and compressed by too many obligations, instead, I have more space to breathe and *be* and genuinely enjoy my work.

And my grief has now been allowed to come out however it needs—small trickles, waves that suck me in, sometimes at the least expected times. But the gift in all of this is that I have had the space to go where my grief leads me. My life is now so open that I don't have to shove grief down or cram it aside or dissociate it in order to do life. I just have to show up for me.

And in so doing, what I have begun to see is that the part of me that needed healing is perhaps the healer herself. That somewhere along the way I got a definition of what it meant to "be a healer" that no longer fits, and is actually holding me back from doing the true healing work I am called to do.

An image came up in a channeling I received back at the beginning of the new year. The image is of me in a pool with 2x4's on my shoulders, and I am carrying people on them, all as I try to stay afloat. *This was you back in Anchorage,* I am told. The image then shifted where the 2x4's are smaller, the pool remains, but there are no longer people. *This is you right now,* I am told.

What does all this mean, I ask?

You need to learn to get out of the pool.

What does it mean to get out of the pool? It's a conundrum, and I contemplate this question over the winter months. I completely relate to the first image with all the people, heavy as it is; I carried a lot back in my Anchorage life, most of it requiring direct contact and direct energetic exchange, and it was eventually too much. But I thought coming to Kauai was my way of releasing those 2x4's and getting out of the pool, and I am jarred by the thought that things could change even further, as I ponder and examine my own relationship to what it means to be a healer.

The wounded healer is the healer who knows both sides of the wound. Who at some point in life is pierced by something beyond their current framework and world of self; and that piercing causes them to expand beyond those frameworks and search for answers and information that transcends their own being. The wound acts as a gateway to a greater depth and spirituality, and they travel through great darkness in order to find what they need to bring light into the space.

The wounded healer learns to transcend the limitations of self and find a Higher Perspective, and as the healer learns to heal their own wound, they become the sunlight healer, turning around and helping others start to heal.

I am not afraid of emotional pain. I am not afraid to sit with people in the darkness. When I was in the worst of my grief over Brent, I never feared the depth and black that was there, though I certainly didn't savor it. My relationship to healing has been one that was forged through being the wounded healer, and my belief that Love acts as both wound and balm. Hardship comes into our lives as a way to crack us open, make us bigger and wider than we were before, so we grow and understand a greater depth of humanity and spirituality, bringing a wider expanse of love, empathy, and compassion into our lives.

I have had many wounds in my time as a healer, but it was my divorce back in 2011 that really set me on this path. My world was shattered, and I fractured with it, and who I was at the end of that journey was very different than who I was before. Shamanism might call it a dismemberment or dissolution, I was ripped apart piece by piece, the old me dissolved, and when I was finally stitched back together, I had learned lessons of love on my journey that created the foundation and framework of who I became. At the time, I felt born anew and called to walk a deeper path of Love.

That foundation continued to get sturdier over the next few years every time I went through hardship and pain and found new ways to choose love. I was single at the time and saw time as a resource I had in abundance. I gave freely of myself and often. Without realizing I was doing it, I set myself up in a position of being needed, and began to equate being needed with being of service, with being loved, *with being good*.

It didn't matter that sometimes I felt fried to a crisp. That my own energy field felt drained and depleted. Just like somebody who keeps getting sick with the same virus, because they never rest long enough to give their system time to fully recover, I never gave myself time to fully recover from the massive amount of energy I expended in my healing work. People seemed to need me, I felt responsible, and I struggled with saying "no."

Then I met my husband, and his presence in my life challenged me to look at myself differently. When he moved to Alaska, it was an incredible jolt when he told me living with me was like living with two different people. The weekday BethAnne, who would come home from her practice at the end of the day drained, cranky, zombie-like, and so worn out I was almost mute. And the weekend BethAnne who was my usual affable, open self.

My husband was the beginning of my change in my relationship with healing. I started to see I was expending energy at a rate I couldn't refuel, and that I needed to make changes. I started to work less. I tried harder to say "no," though I often wasn't successful—it can be very difficult to pop yourself out of the patterns you always said "yes" to when people are used to those yeses. But still, I made strides in reworking my relationship with being a healer, and I began to identify within myself a woman who wanted to take a step back from always doing one on one healing and reach people in a greater capacity.

And then Brent happened, and I felt like I had to carry on. Quite truthfully, I don't know that I would have stopped my practice given the choice, it's who I was and all I knew to do. I found solace in being there for others, in my ability to still lend healing energy, even as I needed healing energy myself and was forced to find it through nature, spirit, and solitude.

But something happened during that season in life where I began to wonder if I was too good at what I did. How was it that I was holding everything together? Wouldn't it be more normal and human to simply fall apart? It was like I'd learned the art of healing so well, I couldn't help but do it when put in that space, even though part of me was crying out to be healed. But I took my grief and began to transform it, offer it up to others for their healing. *Because I am the wounded healer, and that is what I knew to do.*

As I sit in Kauai, looking out at the jungle green, listening to the rooster's crow, and seeing a pale blue drift of clouds travel by, I can honestly say that I did what anybody would have done in that situation: I did the best I could. And it wasn't right or wrong or anything other than what it is—a reflection of where my life was at the time. *I did what I knew to do. I was the person I knew to be.* I wouldn't have done anything differently, as I see the path I've walked, what came of it, and I am blessed by my former practice and the people I worked with and all they taught me along the way.

I was who I was then, and I am who I am now. A woman who came to this island for change for multiple reasons, one of the biggest being that things were incredibly out of balance in my life. My relationship with healing had become out of balance. My relationship to equating my worth with being needed was out of balance.

I think on all these things as I tread water in that pool. Contemplating what it means to get out of the pool. Contemplating a paradigm shift and wondering what that even looks like. Contemplating the idea that if all I did with the rest of my life was work at a coffee shop, in the eyes of Spirit I would be just as loved, just as beautiful, just as worthy, and just as valued as I am when I'm doing my healing work.

That who I am isn't dictated by what I do and by my doing, it is dictated by who I am and by my being.

As somebody who has identified with the path of the wounded healer for years, who dedicated so much time and energy to the path of being a healer, I am stepping back and trying to lean into this paradigm shift and find new ways of being, of healing, as I've come to reflect on my life and realize:

My own relationship with healing has become the wound.

98

SELF-FORGIVENESS

THERE IS GOING to come a point in time where you may start to realize that hanging on to the past and hanging on to your past mistakes is no longer serving you—and I hope we all get to that point sooner rather than later, as life is quite short and precious, and each of us is imperfect. And so in those imperfections, we don't always get it right moment to moment.

And when we come to those places in our lives, where we didn't get it right, the best we can do is make amends in the ways available to us. Maybe we go to the person and apologize. Maybe we just send the energy of humble, apologetic intent to the situation or individual, and ask the universe to direct that energy to where it needs to go. Trusting that the soft pink light of forgiveness and letting go can happen at any point in time—when we finally feel ready to let go.

But more than anything, when we bump into the spots where we feel we failed, we need to find a way to make amends with ourselves. We need to find a way to forgive the times we may have been foolish or insensitive or hurtful or wrong. We're really only meant to hang onto that stuff long enough to learn our lessons and integrate the heart truths that come from the situation.

After that, there is nothing new to do or to learn in our old territory, and so hanging onto it and rehearsing it will only leave us repeating old patterns, acting out, and projecting our own stuff onto others, instead of simply owning it. Creating a dead end street that only leads to a sense of going backwards and being mired in the past.

And we are not meant to be stuck in the past. The past contains old dramas. Old stories. Old lessons. Old shells of self, which keep us from having space to embrace the new. The past is yesterday, and today is NOW, and if we want to be joyful and free, then we have to learn to release our expectation of being "right," and accept that there will be just as many times where we are "wrong."

What it comes down to are the choices we make on a daily basis, and our willingness to acknowledge our part in things without attachment to whether we were right or wrong. Be curious. Do the best you can each day. Learn from yourself. Cultivate an ongoing attitude of forgiveness within; be expected to be surprised at how much space this will free up to forgive others. Become a student of unconditional love; realize this LOVE exists in spades and fistfuls and never-ending quantities simply because you are a child of the universe.

Fight for your right to be happy. Place your hand on your heart and heed its truth: your soul is so much more than your story.

Your soul is so much more than your story.

99

Like pieces of fabric that are wrinkled up
and folded and knotted and then dipped
into tie-dye, maybe life wrinkles and folds and knots us
time and time again:
creating new patterns in the fabric of our soul,
inviting us to a constant state of creative evolution;
helping us live a life of surrender to our own
continual rearrangement.

100

PARADIGM SHIFT

HOW DO YOU go about shifting a paradigm? We develop ways we look at the world: mental templates and constructs our mind organizes information around. When something contradicts or doesn't fit, we are either forced to reevaluate those structures and do some rearranging to create new space, or we reject that which doesn't fit so we aren't faced with the conflict of cognitive dissonance.

Paradigms are based upon layers and layers of values and assumptions. What we're taught about the world and who we're taught to be. What we come to believe about the world and our ideas of who we believe we are. Experiences that shape and mold and create foundations and lenses. More often than not, it takes a lot to shift a paradigm. Usually, the structure we are trying to shift has deep history and roots, and those things are not easily swayed.

Sometimes something smashes into our structure, and the shift begins instantly and involuntarily—life forces our hand and we are forced to find change. Then there are other times where we know we are seeking a new way of thinking or of being, but since we haven't discovered what yet, we don't know how to make that shift. We just know that we feel stuck and something needs to change. There's no timeline for this process as our psyche and subconscious and mental constructs have their own sense of time and arrangement, and it can take a while for our heart and soul knowledge to hook up to the rest of us.

When you are in this space, others may not understand what you are trying to do, as they're not experiencing your drive for change. They may even want you to return to the old you, as that version of self was more comfortable for them. But when you're the one going through it, you don't want to return to the old you. You've become uncomfortable with what was once comfortable, and so you are seeking and searching and hungering for something different.

A new way of being. A new way of doing. A new concept of self. A new relationship with life. Something that more fully supports your own personal evolution and growth and gives you space to actualize who you're becoming.

Sometimes you have to find a way to turn your own self upside down. To shake up and shake out your preconceived notions. To undergo a radical rearrangement where you're not afraid to surrender to life's process of change. To rattle your own cages so hard you finally figure out how to pop yourself out of the bars. You'll find yourself standing on new ground and so much space will have opened up that you are no longer afraid to challenge your old assumptions, your old ways, your old cage.

And you'll gradually begin to realize the biggest thing that was always keeping you from freeing yourself—was you.

101

COMPASS

Roosters sing
to island breeze,
orange flowers sway
and green leaves speak.

They teach me what
it means to be,
no more, no less,
just pared down me.

Who doesn't have to
do anything or
try anything or
say anything or
be something else
to be valued and seen—

Except live the Love
I have inside,
and trust it to direct me
wherever it heeds.

102

NOODLES

YESTERDAY WAS NATIONAL Siblings Day; it's a strange day for me, one that would probably pass unnoticed if not for all the posts on social media. Three years ago, I had mixed feelings on this day—Brent and I were not in a good place, he was going through some dark times, and it impacted our relationship. I grieved not having a better relationship.

Two years ago, I was in pain on this day. I grieved the loss of my brother. I grieved Brent. I grieved us. I grieved the cracks and breaks in this world, and how difficult it can be to reach for love in this place. All those pictures of happy siblings seemed to mock my loss; I was so close to the heart of grief my lungs were crushed by all the reminders.

Last year, I shared a picture of both of us on this day. It felt good and it felt right. I was over a year into my grief journey, and I was at a space of profound love for who Brent had been, who we had been—the beautiful parts of us and even the rough parts. And I had a sense of who he was in the afterlife and an ongoing connection to him; sharing a picture felt natural and authentic.

This year, I felt numb to the whole thing, except I know I wasn't really numb, there is always something lurking beneath a numb feeling—we're just usually not ready to access or process the information. It wasn't on my heart to share a picture, the gesture felt empty. And it wasn't on my heart to write a reflection, no words were flowing.

So I did nothing; I felt detached.

Then today I was struck by the thought—*I don't want to share some crappy picture we took years ago.* I don't want to share some old memory, because now all I have are old memories. I don't want to share some pictures I've already shared before. Brent didn't like taking pictures, so most of the pictures I have of us later in life are ones taken on this island when we were here over the holidays and I made him take selfies with me.

There are precious few of those.

And I don't want to recycle one of those again. I want a new picture.

Sometimes I still hate the realization there are no new pictures; there will be no new pictures.

The nature of life is transient; we all know change is life's way, yet it is so difficult to accept. Painful to accept. Death being the most painful of lessons. And even though I look at Brent's death as a rebirth into the spirit world, the fact is: he is no longer physically present in this world. And sometimes that absence aches in ways I can't explain.

Even as a writer and a psychologist, sometimes I have no words for my grief, and I am left sinking into my own murky, confusing experience of self and just feeling my way through.

Grief is a strange beast. It's twisty, not linear. Like a bowl of noodles where everything gets whirled and twirled together, chasing each other, weaving in and out in a cluster of slippery swirls. So it is with grief, our experience of it swerving and curving, twisting and taking us on emotional detours whose destination we didn't anticipate.

It's so utterly human to want a new picture. It feels like a younger part of myself, more adolescent, rebellious, less accepting. She wants to stomp her feet at having to be grown up and wise, at having to accept the things that have come to pass. She doesn't want to make the best of the old memories and find the good and find perspective.

She wants new memories.

She is part of who I am, and though she doesn't really run the ship—I try to reserve that position for my wise self—she's on the ship, and her young, human hurt informs my heart and soul. It is worthy of recognition and honor.

Grief taps into us on multidimensional layers, intersecting in multiple places across our own timeline. It can make you feel very young and childlike, like a little kid who just wants to cry and scream "not fair, not fair, not fair." It can also make you feel ancient, like your heart holds the heavy stories of a thousand-year-old grove. There's not a single emotion grief doesn't tap; you never know what you are going to get in that bowl; each noodle being a part of the whole, each noodle equally valid and simply one more expression of the love that underlies the loss.

It is a new day today, I stepped away from these words since I wrote that last paragraph. That younger part of me said, "I don't want to write about this right now." So instead, I took a nap, a break from writing, and gave allowance to my feelings so they could be whatever they needed to be.

Somewhere in the middle of all of that Brent dropped by. We journeyed back into the kitchen of our childhood home on a Friday night. Melted large spoonfuls of butter on a fresh pot of noodles with Dad's special sauce; our parents close by, all of us getting ready to watch a movie together. The memory makes me smile.

Smile Little Sister. Smile. I promise you we'll make new memories. They'll just be a little different now.

It makes me remember you can't build a home out of grief. There is no joy there. You can only examine the tangles of grief as they come your way. Do your best to be open and honest with each strand. Acknowledge it as valid. Release it when ready.

Then keep on pressing forward, doing your best to be here now and find the joy.

103

THE PLACES JOY LIVES

J OY WILL SPONTANEOUSLY find us at times, but more often than not, I think we have to find it by developing an eye for it, where we take the time to see the spaces that joy already is living. The love of an old dog. The beauty of fresh flowers. The cheerful color of daffodil yellow. Fluffy things. New sky and moonlight. Taking time to count our blessings. *Meaning it.* Soft sheets and naps. Fresh breezes and warm mugs of comfort drink. Monster cookies. Rainbows. Finding any cause to celebrate. The mood boost you get when you smile.

Somewhere along the way, we lose our childlike sense of wonder and delight. Adulthood can be heavy and joy seems a silly luxury, and yet the energy of joy is holy energy. It makes us feel lighter. Brighter. More at peace and at ease. We laugh more and wherever there is laughter there is always Love. We feel more connected in those moments and are able to transcend the drama of this world and our own mental chatter, as the energy of joy invites us to appreciate and BE.

Be in the moment. Focus on the good. Notice what matters. Notice the good things already surrounding you and cultivate the energy of the feelings that come from those good things. And in those moments of being, we are given the invitation to remember joy is our birthright and our natural state of soul. And so every time we tap into its radiant energy of light—we are in essence returning home.

104

THE SLEEPING GIANT

THE SUN IS shining after weeks of rain; it is a welcome relief to see it streaming through the tall pine trees. It's hot on the mountain today, I'm hiking at what has become one of my favorite places and safe harbors. The Sleeping Giant is a mountain close to my house, I hiked it years ago when Brent and I first started coming over to the island with my parents, never dreaming I would some day not only live on this island, but live eight minutes away from the trail.

Now, I come here regularly, and I know the trail quite well. The red dirt that can either be tacky and sticky or a total mudslide depending on weather; the holy tree cathedral, which makes one pause in awesome wonder; the giant old power stone where flowers are often laid out in offering; the view from the top which looks out over the east side and coast. There are many sacred places on this trail if you know how to open your heart and listen.

Today's hike is spontaneous. I feel the sudden urge to go to the mountain after my last client, and I've got a happy, wagging Frodo running back and forth who seems pleased with my decision. I have found that the longer you return to the same places in nature, the more you develop a relationship with the land.

I've been coming here fairly regularly since we moved, so by now I'd told this mountain most of my joys, troubles, and secrets. She always reassures me that she is big enough to hold them, and in turn blesses me by drawing my attention to something I previously missed: a cluster of pink flowers, an area among her pines that feels extra potent with grace; calmer thoughts and new ideas; deeper encounters with Spirit, as its easier to *hear* in wild places.

One day I kept finding bright red petals along her trail, and when I reached the top instead of going to my favorite look out, I followed a little side trail I never go down, only to find an arch in the stone foundation that looked out over the ocean with a bouquet of red flowers that had been placed there. Whoever brought those flowers up had done so out of love, and so I just sat there in that space of beauty and love and let myself be consecrated by its gentle energy.

On this day, nothing quite so grand has happened yet. I'm just happy to be out there in the sunshine, and I revel in having the space to be in this moment on a Thursday afternoon, the kind of space I never had back in Alaska with my busy schedule. The top is windy, a welcome relief from the 80–degree temperatures, which tell me summer weather may soon be here. I notice the turquoise blue of the sky and the cerulean of the sea. The emerald of the jungle and the purity of the white egrets flying by.

And then Brent is there with me. He's been on my mind often this day, it's Thursday—the day of the week named after the Greek god Thor—and as *Thor* was one of his favorite movies, I've noticed he has a penchant for dropping by on Thursdays. But if he's been close by today, this is the first he's made his presence known. I can feel him in the wind in that moment. I know it's him, because I get that deep feeling of resonance that comes over me when he's close: it's like a gorgeous musical composition is being played on my inner piano, and the sounds echo through my chambers making me feel everything is beautiful and wonderful and exactly as it should be.

Why have you brought me up here?, I say to him, as I now realize he's the reason I felt prompted and compelled to spontaneously go hike in the first place.

I brought you up for pleasure, he says. *Because you deserve to feel pleasure Little Sister.*

Pleasure, I roll the word around on my tongue as I consider the things that bring me pleasure. Any time I see a rainbow. Watching the clouds form and reform. Sunrise and sunset. Good cream in my coffee. Cheese platters and candles on a cozy, rainy night. Waking up before anybody else in the family and looking at my husband and our three fur kids cuddled up in bed. French fries. White wine. Time to write and daydream and introspect. Salty ocean air and moonlight.

There's nothing fancy on the list. All of it is easily available. I notice that nowhere on that list is anything having to do with the bigger identity and life purpose questions that I've been sifting through in my heart. The answers to those questions lay somewhere else, but not on my list of pleasures. It makes me think how the world would be different if more people lived joyfully, savoring pleasure. How we might treat each other differently, how much lighter things may feel, how people may start to spontaneously heal their own emotional wounds and scars through the simple act of intentional appreciation, pleasure, and gratitude.

Brent and the mountain have given me a great gift this day. Greater than I can fathom in the moment, as the complicated knots of my ongoing question—*how do I heal my relationship with healing?*— has just unraveled a little bit further.

Brent stays close by a little while longer, but as more people come up the mountain and reach the top, I can feel he's getting further away and the spell of the moment has been broken. Frodo sits faithfully by my feet, staring out at the view, as I take another few minutes to just be in this moment of receptivity. Watching the blue and green of this island dance, thinking about what brings me joy, getting ready to head back down the mountain; smiling with this blessing.

105

SILVER SKY

S OMEWHERE IN THE seams of spring's days, I'm letting myself reform under the gleam of silver sky.
Let the oceans help me breathe, let the rains wash clean, let the new blooms encourage my heart to seed and be a freer version of me. Allow old values to drift away: I don't need to be needed to be loved, or equate a checklist with being good, or fix each broken wing I see. It is enough to be and hold space for joy, and embody the Love that I seek.

Red mud mixes with tea leaf's green, songbirds meet on the silvery breeze. Chimeral clouds brush the pinks of angel wings, and the earth begins to blossom with soft growth and harmony. And somewhere in the seams of spring's days, I let myself reform under the gleam of silver sky.

Release the shapes of former *me's*, redraw the map of who I'd like to be, relinquish old identities, flip onto my back and float in the pool for a time. Guava berries bud in cherry reds and leafy limes, the sodden earth saturates with mists and tempest's night. Moon illuminates her subtle phases and lines, as season shifts its paradigm.

Inviting a greater depth of believing, winter's deep sleep waking up to new freeing, the road to becoming is paved with new seeing— *Life is a constant rearrangement of being.* And somewhere in the seams of spring's days, I let myself reform under the gleam of silver sky.

106

EXPERTS

I CAN'T STOP BEING me, just because somebody doesn't understand me. Just as you can't stop being you because somebody doesn't understand you. We need to be ourselves in this life—it is the only path to authenticity there is.

Trying to stoop lower and reduce yourself to meet somebody where they are at will only serve in making you small. Just as trying to reach down, do the work for them, and pull somebody up to meet you where you are at will only make you realize how tiring it is to carry somebody.

We are who we are and where we are, each of us navigating our paths according to our own dictates of heart and soul, and so it becomes important to recognize those who have a parallel journey we're meant to walk beside, and those whose paths split from ours, each of us free to move in the direction that resonates.

I believe this is one of the hardest lessons to learn in life. To grow beyond a model where we seek other's validation and approval. To do the work of self so diligently that we turn inwards when our buttons get pressed, and instead of saying *how can they act like that?* we learn to say *what is this triggering inside of me and how can I bring healing to this space.* To find the courage to simply be ourselves and to find the courage to let others do the same, recognizing this as a two-fold process of courage.

Because it does take courage to let go. It does take courage to recognize others will see you through a distorted lens and that you may see them through a distorted lens. That you can't do a thing about the cloudiness of their lens, but you can work to keep yours clean and let those times it clouds become a teacher.

We must do this work in order to free ourselves. In order to embody ourselves and learn to be our own experts. And as time goes on, those that don't understand you may still sting or hurt or ache a bit, but the benefits gained from walking your own path will become so great you wouldn't want to go back.

And any words of dissuasion that others may say will begin to pale in lieu of the magnificence of *you* claiming your own brilliant light.

107

TRANSCENDENTAL PSYCHOLOGY

AFTER AN INITIAL burst of sun, which welcomed the spring and seemed to hint of summer, the island is fraught with storms, monsoons, and gray. We've been told that the amount of rain we've had this year is highly unusual for Kauai; flash floods, an almost constant gray, and bursts of rain ranging from fine mists to heavy sheets have blanketed the sky more often than not for months.

Though I'm ready for more sunshine and balmier weather, I try to find the gifts. The rain lends a mystery to things, and as I'm still untangling the mysteries of myself and my next step, it supports that process.

I pull out old art journals and let those inspire me to keep creating new art. I smile fondly at the girl from 2012, fresh out of a divorce, who worked so hard to cultivate an internal sense of love, peace, joy, and light. My old mysteries lay within those pages; I often had a burgeoning sense I was moving towards something greater in my life, though I couldn't see it, and I learned to trust the course anyways.

My old journals remind me where it all started and where so much of who I've become began. It's like a blessing from my younger self, who's standing back in 2012, looking into the future, smiling with joy, and saying, *I knew we could do it. Don't give up. I believe in us.* They encourage me to whittle and chisel away at my children's books and consider new artistic endeavors.

I begin to utilize my intuitive gifts in new ways. I open myself up to intuiting where I can and what I can, wrapping the process in love and seeing what comes through. I channel on the energy of love, creativity, nature, joy, the energy of any given day—there is always something new and beautiful to learn. I begin to see/feel/perceive even more subtle nuances for how information comes through, as well as get a deepening sense of spiritual presence.

I write and I work on *Transformations of The Sun,* I see how much of what I've already written this past year folds so beautifully into the manuscript, and I marvel at the thought that somehow my soul always knew I'd be writing this book, even if my consciousness didn't know it yet. I realize it's like I've been writing it without knowing I was writing it all along, and I'm astounded at how quickly it flies together.

I consider how to move forward and unify my intuitive and spiritual side with my psychology side. Because I've realized I will forever be a Psychologist at my roots. Ever since I declared my degree in college, I've been in the field. I bulldozed my way through graduate school condensing a 5–year program into 4, and was standing with my doctorate in hand at the age of 26.

That journey began 20 years ago, and I see how much of myself developed around the anchor of my psychology degree, my background in trauma therapy, and all those years in practice. I didn't need to rid myself of that part of me after all, I just needed to set her aside for a while, so other pieces had room to grow.

And those pieces did grow to help me transcend my old space of self. They just needed a bit of time, nourishment, and TLC to help grow them bigger, name them, and claim them. Intuitive. Channeler. Artist. Writer. Author. Mystic. Creative. These are all pieces of me and this past year has been about letting each of those crystallize and actualize so they feel like more solid components of my identity.

I begin to realize on a more profound level that everything I've passed through to get me here, the things I've felt drawn to, the dreams of my younger self, and the notions and ideas and seedlings of visions have all been stored inside of me helping me to create a platform to be here, at this space in time, and grow into a new version of self who can fully bloom.

Seeing as how I've transcended who I once was I see a new path: Transcendental Psychology. I'm not quite sure how the finished structure will look, but I know what I want it to house: a multidimensional approach to healing, which holds more space for Love, Spirit and Creativity. A space that is less focused on this being my *work* and more focused on this being my *joy* and helping others find their joy.

Because as I've sat with my relationship with healing I have come to see that I made healing work. And sometimes it is work and work is necessary—there is nothing glamorous about rolling up your sleeves and digging through your own mud to find your diamonds and pearls.

But I have also come to see that there are other ways to bring healing to this world, which encompass more joy.

Healing can take place as I sit in a coffee shop and channel the energy of love, send it out to everyone around me.

Healing can take place walking down the street, smiling at others, saying hello with warmth and sincerity.

Healing can take place with my clients, and I can tap into deeper levels of truth to help them see behind the scenes in their own life.

Healing can take place in my writing and my art and the color I bring to this world.

Healing can take place sitting on top of a mountain, thinking kind thoughts, and sending those out into the world.

Healing doesn't have to be something I *do*. Healing is something I can *be*. Because when you are in alignment and in joy with yourself and with life, you and your energy can't help but be a conduit for healing the spaces around you. I don't have to do anything, I just have to be and trust Life to help me sort out the rest. I finally begin to see what my mentor has been telling me for years: You are the library, and you take your books of medicine with you wherever you go. You don't have to Do anything, it's all in your Being.

Your very act of being itself becomes the medicine that helps bring healing to the world.

108

YOU ARE THE ART

We collect pieces of ourselves as we go. Clues and cues and tiny gems and treasures, which we tuck away until it's time to unfold a fuller story of self. The soul leaves cake crumbs to help us follow the path.

That poem you wrote years back may one day become part of a book. That strange sense of restlessness you felt months ago may have been the first stirrings and dawnings of a new invitation for growth. That vision you once had of yourself doing something different than what you do now may some day come into fruition, and if you just stay with it and let that part of yourself emerge, you'll eventually find your own brand of artistry.

Each scrap and pearl and shell and tiny pebble, each little bit you discover each day, is a piece of the greater mosaic of you.

Wings don't unfurl over night. They start to develop in the cocoon, and sometimes you may not even realize you've been in a cocoon until you're ready to break through its silken strands of incubation.

A heart can change in a beat; and you never know what might change your heart.

You may feel directionless one lunar cycle, unable to see your bigger picture, then find your deeper clarity somewhere between the moon's next wax and wane.

The feelings and insights and dreams and heart states we sometimes dismiss, disregard, discount, because we don't understand them, are often inklings of soul helping us paint our fuller picture. They don't always have to make sense, they are here to help us delve deeper into our own mysteries, so one can better know their depths.

There can be a lot of layers to dig through to get to your depths. Tiers and stripes and stratums of sediment built up through the years of who and how and what this world told you to be. But underneath all that is your authenticity, your essence, your diamonds of truth, which can only be found in your deep.

So don't distrust yourself. Or discredit your dreams. Or dismiss the pieces of you that you are slowly gathering, even if you don't entirely understand them. You are drawn to them for a reason; they resonate in your heart. Because each color and line and shade and tone is working to create a fuller picture of you—

Your soul is your canvas and you are the art.

109

ALOE

My dear one,
don't let them get
you down.

This world can be
a reckless place,
filled with bruises
and rough hands.

And your heart is
soft; a tender
soapstone meant
for gentle echoes,
not harsh noise.

It doesn't get
any easier—zipping
that fragile skin each
time it wants to collapse,
but I can tell you this:
it is that tender fragility
that makes you
unique.

For you are a light,
in a world dripped in dark;
your softness burns
with the juice of the stars
who squeezed their
magic into you.

You don't need to fit,
you just need to be you,
let that tender heart pour
into yourself every time
you feel bruised—

For love is the aloe
to heal the wound,
and you my dear walk
with the soul of love's truth.

110

How to Know Your Soul

You have to keep showing up for yourself. Again and again and again. Show up and do your own work of heart and mind and spirit. Learn how to sit in silence and know yourself. Learn how to breathe through your uncertainty.

Realize all experiences of yourself are right and good and valid.

Learn what works for you until you become your own guru on you. Learn how to cultivate discernment and wisdom. Learn to differentiate between what the world says you should be and who you feel called to be.

Realize all experiences of yourself are right and good and valid.

Discover that if it doesn't resonate with you then it is not for you. Realize that you don't have to be anyone special. You don't have to do anything special. You don't have to search so hard for the answers—you just have to learn how to be yourself.

Realize all experiences of yourself are right and good and valid.

Do this and you cannot help but find the soul directed path—your soul directed path. Do this and you will quickly begin to learn what is right for you and what isn't. Do this and you will begin to see you always had the answers—written inside the depths of your heart—waiting for you to look within so you could remember what is true.

Realize all experiences of yourself are right and good and valid.

There isn't a single person out there who is going to show up, roll up their sleeves, and do the work for you. Who can tell you how to live or what your truth is or the things that will light your heart most bright. It is just that easy and just that hard: to know your soul you must cast off all that this world has told you about who you should be, then get down to the business of finding your truth.

Realizing all experiences of yourself are right and good and valid—the language of your soul only you can discover for you.

111

THE PLACE WHERE INTROVERTS GO

SOMETIMES I HAVE to go quiet for a while, and go to that place where introverts go. Where alone becomes necessity and silver silence my soulful gold.

Sometimes I have no words for a while, for I've gone to the place where grievers meet. Tears are the language that transfigures our ache, for sometimes this world is too harsh to speak.

Sometimes I have to go in for a while, and return to the space of soul's intelligence. I retreat to the turquoise cave of my heart, an oasis of peace in a world that makes no sense.

Sometimes I need my space for a while, to be in the place where the empath feels. To let my heart break on the shores of this world and spend myself out on humanity's fields.

Sometimes I need *need* for a while. To be in the void where love and loss link. To let myself drift on the seas of this life, dissolve in their mists as I hunger for drink.

Sometimes I need be for a while. To be okay with this human mess. Where grace is the blanket that covers life's wounds, and I can curl up in her folds and find rest.

112

LABYRINTH

G RIEF IS AN amorphous language I'll be learning to speak the rest of my life. New words and new phraseology forever being introduced; old words that I thought I had memorized suddenly shifting and changing in composition or accentuation.

I think this is part of what makes grief so complex—there are all these tiers and layers and dimensions to it, and you can warp throughout these dimensions multiple times in a day. That's why it's so nuanced: it's a labyrinth with many levels, twists, and turns—that keep changing—and at times, it can feel impossible to find your way out or make sense of the passages.

Some days that labyrinth feels less complex, but there are other days where I still find myself wandering in it. One moment I'll travel to the deep, desolate mud of earth's crust then I'm on to the sorrow of sad, lonely ocean waves only to find myself transported up into the dissolution of the clouds, drifting and lost.

Then I'll time warp back to 1980 when we were little kids, and life was simple: cartoons, the sandbox, Mom's meatloaf, trips to our Methodist church, Dad driving us in the car while the soundtrack to "Sound of Music" plays on. Because those who traverse grief's labyrinth are also time travelers, able to cross great spaces and spans in mere seconds and breaths and heart beats. You don't really know when you might be called to travel or where or when you'll return from the journey.

And the only thing that I have found that helps you make your way through that labyrinth is Love. Because Love isn't linear, there is no start and finish to it. Love exists always. Circular, infinite, limitless, enduring, eternal. Transcendent. Which means no matter what layer or tier or time you find yourself at, Love is there.

Enfolding us, helping us, guiding us, holding our hand, and lighting our path. Reminding us that the only reason we find ourselves in the labyrinth in the first place is because we loved. And when we tap into Love we automatically create a doorway we can step through, so no matter how lost you feel—

Love will always help you find a way to return to your home.

113

ANTIDOTE

I am numb
heart muscles limp
tears all spent
from
feeling
and feeling
and feeling.

There are times
where the grooves
of grief
carve so far into
my deep,
I don't think I will
ever straighten them out
or remember
what it
feels to *feel*
"normal."

And then I remember:
somewhere around
the coordinates
of
I don't think I can take
it anymore
and
compassion
and
humanity
and

Love—
that if you are living
awake
and alive
in this world,
"normal"
is not meant
for you.

And the hurt
that clings
to the cut of
soul's deep
—empathy's antidote to ambivalence and apathy—
is the very stuff
that is going
to help heal
help feel
help fill
our world.

114

You have to learn to make
the energy of love
what shields you and what reveals you.
That is the only thing I have found
that helps me stay open
in a world that often
makes me want to close.

115

Non-Sequitur

THE LONGER I deepen my relationship with grief, the more I realize that grief truly is a non-sequitur. We live out its irresolution the rest of our lives and our being, and breathing, and loving becomes the resolution, even as the missing and nonsensical never fit.

I still miss Brent every single day. Not a day goes by where I don't think about him, or have this ancient sense of awareness of how losing him altered me. I know exactly how I got from point A to point Z, even as some days I still wonder how I got from point A to point Z.

Some things in life are like that. Irresolute. They don't fit neatly into a bundle. They don't logically add up with a conclusion that makes sense. Their emotional experience cannot be contained or quantified or reduced to a model. They are what they are; tangents and detours and traumas and unfinished stories with ongoing questions, whose answers we seek through our living.

I lived all the words in the pages of this book and have tried to convey them to the best of my ability—tell the story of who I became after losing Brent. Of what happened next. Of grief and love's transformative effects.

This book tells a whole story whose strands weave together into my own evolution, and yet it's like there is another timeline that still plays out in my mind. It's the timeline of what would be if Brent hadn't died. It's a timeline where back on that January day the only news I got on my phone from my parents was "we've got dinner waiting back at the condo" instead of "you need to call us ASAP."

Who would that BethAnne have become? And who would Brent have become had he lived out his life down here?

I will never know, and there are days—even as I hold the awareness and acceptance of what did happen in my heart—that the answers to that other story pull at my heart. There is still a sense of abrupt departure. A ripping. A quantum leap. A life ended too soon, which forced my life as I knew it to end too, morphing me into who I am now.

I will never know those answers. Time may bring more peace to my questions, but perhaps it won't, and I'll continue to smack into those questions, which sometimes still startle and jar me and leave me saying, "is this really my life?" Perhaps those questions will always be a part of me, and I just have to keep making peace with the fact that some questions are unanswerable.

At least on this side of the door.

Going through grief has taught me that you can't find a resolution in the middle of irresolution. Sometimes all you can do is press pause, and recognize the disjointed Salvador Dali-esque surreality of this life, and just make space for it to be what it is.

Grief has taken on a softer tone the further I step from the deepest point of the pain. It used to be a flashing neon sign, placed directly by heart's window, glaring and jolting and waking me from the slumber of my life prior to losing Brent; my awareness was fully centered on that intrusive, blinking light. And it no longer feels like that, except on rare occasions where it creeps up on me and surprises me, and I surrender the day to it.

It's different now; subdued. It's settled into my joints more; settled into my cells. It's become part of my story and part of who I am, giving me an underlying sense of sorrow even as it heightens and sweetens, making me so thankful for the journey that is my life.

And the love I've lived out during this journey has continued to grow exponentially. It is a love so strong that it gave me the courage to make my grief journey with openness and naked vulnerability. It is a love so strong that it gave me the courage to love harder, even in the heart of my loss. It is a love that took me on a leap of faith to this beautiful island of magic, green, and sea.

It is a love that altered who I am spiritually, chiseling away at sharp human edges, hollowing me out through faith and trust, so something greater could come in. It is a love that reached through the door; that crossed the threshold of infinity; that created a channel to other worlds, so more Love and Peace and Grace and Compassion could be brought into this one to help heal the planet at this time.

It is a Love transcendent.

And I have Brent to thank for that. Maybe his death will always feel like a non-sequitur, like the story doesn't add up, the conclusion an irresolution. But the love I've found as I've carried him inside has become my solution and my salvation. It made me so much more than who I was before.

And for that, I am grateful.

116

FINDING BRENT

Sometimes he feels so close I lift my hand towards the sky, as if we are all in a giant bubble and the other side is right there—just a breath away—and he is lifting his hand and reaching back…pressing, pressing, pressing. The veil is but a wisp of illusion. One of these days I will find a way to reach through. —FROM LAMENTATIONS OF THE SEA

I T'S THURSDAY AND Brent is close by. I can feel him so strongly today, I keep expecting him to appear in front of me, but of course, as always I can't see him, I only *feel* him.

He seems strangely quiet, though quite present. And I realize with frustration that Brent seems to have his own time for when he speaks, and I hear him. Or maybe it's not Brent's time, maybe it's just sometimes that I'm more clear and better able to listen. Either way, it's inconsistent, and it flashes in my mind that I wish I could create a better channel so I could communicate with him and better hear.

It's in my heart to have clearer contact, though I don't know how to do it. But I speak my heart into the space of the open room and just ask—*Help me understand how I can hear you more clearly.*

It's the kind of day where I can tell something is going to happen. My angel tingles are extra tingly. My cells feel like they're vibrating. The air itself feels electric and sparkly; little white lights keep flashing across my periphery, and I head to the beach with a sense of purpose as I mull over the idea of how to reach him.

It's gray and windy, a storm has been sweeping through the island, and the storm energy matches my swishes and whooshes and tingles as I drive and contemplate, while the radio plays "Lean On Me." *Just call me, if you need a friend. Call me. Call me. Call me. Call me. Just Call me.*

The lyrics keep repeating over and over, "call me, call me, call me." And I feel like I could fall out of my car, as my heart leaps and my voice catches, and I realize I'm being given a message. It never occurred to me to intentionally contact Brent, I'm not a medium, it's not how my gift usually works. I search for him in my mind sometimes and can get a sense of him, and he shows up at other times when I'm working with Spirit, but most of the time he just shows up on his own accord, and I've never truly tried to call him for the sole purpose of contact.

I park at the beach and the hazy sky feels all crisp and zippy as I sit down and settle by the ocean. It's one of those moments where you can feel something extraordinary is about to happen, but you don't know what and you're expectant and almost nervous with anticipation. I know it will work, there is a sense of rightness of moment and perfect alignment. I am *Harry Potter* in this moment, and I just drank my bottle of *Felix Felicius*, liquid luck, and there is a sense of certainty, synchronicity, and intentionality to my movement.

I open myself up, wrap myself in love, and focus as specifically as I can on channeling Brent, asking to speak to him directly in a way that is clear and concise with purity of intent. I'm trying to make a telephone call to eternity, and on this day, *this lucky day*, I know that he is going to pick up on the other end.

All of the sudden there is so much bright. My eyes are closed, and I still feel blinded. It's Brent, and I can see him in my mind's eye as a giant light being. I can't describe it any better than to say he feels huge, uncontainable, and the light is staggering in magnificence. And there is so much love, I feel like a giant balloon expanding with it as I feel my heart stretch and swell.

There is angelic presence around him, and, if it's possible, even more bright light. I get the sensation and impression that he is a light worker on the other side, working with the angels, busy helping others still here on the earthly plane. It's almost too much for me to take in, and I can't hold the connection for very long before things start to feel fuzzy and confusing, and I know I have to let it go and bring myself back to the space of the beach.

But Brent is ready for me and he meets me there—not in his terrific brightness and light body—but with a sense of his presence that's easier for me to perceive.

Brent, help me understand what I just saw, I say. *Help me make sense of these things.*

Two images appear in my mind. One is a student's model of a solar system, the kind you'd see at a science fair back in elementary school: simple, one dimensional, not to scale. The other is an image of the actual solar system: vast, unimaginable and endless in scope.

That's the difference Little Sister, when you think of me and see me, you're usually seeing the model. You just saw the solar system.

He stays for quite a time there on that beach. He speaks through music, songs begin playing on my phone, which resonate with messages on a level so deep I am crying and laughing; I feel so seen and so loved. This space of time is so magical, I don't want it to end. Yet I know we both have lives we need to get back to, and eventually I feel ready to leave the beach, though he still feels close by.

It's not a surprise when *Unchained Melody* comes on the radio later that afternoon at my house, or that I look down to find a shiny penny. I know it's Brent, giving me extra affirmation that he is there, he is real, and I can believe in the veracity of my own experiences. It is enough for now. I had a glimpse of the solar system; one that was too bright for me to hold for too long, because my heart sight and mind's eye wasn't fully ready yet. I'm a first-year piano student trying to play Mozart. I feel my limits, but it is still enough—I've seen the radiant place filled with radiant light where Brent is busy living out his afterlife.

And if I glimpsed it once that means I can do it again. Get stronger. Practice the piano. Learn to play more effortlessly. Learn the subtleties and chords and nuanced rhythms that separate a beginner from an intermediate from an advanced from an expert. I can teach myself to play.

I wrap myself in this knowledge, and in the knowledge that *I did it*. I knew he was out there, I've been sensing him all this time, but now I know so much more. Now I know I can reach him. Now I know that he doesn't always have to be the one who crosses the threshold of the bubble to get to me. Now I know that I can get to him.

Now I know that I finally found a way to reach through.

117

Everywhere

THEY NEVER REALLY leave us. Those who've left too soon.
We find them in each breath, each heartbeat, each laughter,
each joy. They reside there, smiling with us, resting between grace
and gratitude.

Certain songs may come on that tug at the heartstring. Happy
memories may fly, seemingly out of nowhere, into our memory stream.
Birds and butterflies and bunnies act as messengers of spirit speak.
Nature is often a medium to send messages in-between.

We find those we've loved and lost in the creases and folds of
life's fabric, where the veil is thin and permeable. Those moments
when we notice ourselves extra thinking of them, almost hearing a
whisper, catching their scent on the wisps of the wind, seeing them
clearly in mind's eye.

They reach down and tuck us in as we sleep; hover close by singing
the songs of angels. See our tears and gently blow them from our eyes. "I
know you will be okay," they say, "I believe in you. I BELIEVE in YOU."

Unbound by time, unboxed by gravity, freed from the limitations
of this realm; connected to Source where Love is eternal, all things
are possible, and Light is the gracious law guiding the way. They
can be there, while still touching here. Forever carried in our hearts,
forever a soul returned to Love, reaching out through infinity to
remind us they're still with us—

They are always, forever, everywhere.

118

NAUTILUS

I'VE SPENT THE entire day vacillating between wrenching sobs and loony laughter. An email showed up in my inbox this morning saying *Lamentations of The Sea* has won a Silver Nautilus Award in the category of Death & Dying/Grief & Loss.

I couldn't do anything but bawl the first 5 minutes of getting it. Anybody who has ever sacrificed and put their heart, soul, and tears into something that feels like a long shot knows this feeling: it is a culmination and an absolution. And for myself, the first time I actually feel validated as an author.

Seems like I've been on this dark and windy road ever since Brent passed. Following some unseeable force in my heart that keeps pulling me forward. Asking me to take bigger steps of faith, asking me to become a bigger person, inviting me to grow and keep venturing into the unknown, even though I can't see exactly where I am going.

It hit me today just how much I've given up to sit here and write these words. My practice and life in Anchorage was a safety net with a lot of padding; here in Kauai I've often felt I'm teetering upon a narrow ledge, one false step and I'll tumble down and be broken into shambles.

While many have been supportive, I'm not unaware that this life change was met with skepticism by some. Doubts that I can make it as a writer. A dismissal, due to lack of understanding, of my dreams to be an intuitive healer. A dubious disbelief for what looks like a crazy life change that had me giving up all my security to start over and try to make it as an author, creative, and healer.

I understand these thoughts and doubts, I have them too sometimes. Yet every time I come face to face with my shadow doubts, I have had to learn to bring myself back around to a space of trust. Every time I feel like I'm wandering in an empty forest searching for my tribe, still coming up empty, I'm told that Spirit walks with me and when the time is right I'll find the forest has been inhabited by kindreds all along, I just haven't quite reached them yet.

Every time I sit down to write and challenge myself to fierce authenticity and honesty, even as the idle thoughts emerge that people may just think I'm a nutter making all this stuff up about my brother, I push through the thoughts and write my truth anyway. *If there is anything I've learned these last couple of years, it is that we have to set our stories free and breathe them into existence, so they don't crush and suffocate us.*

Lamentations is the first part of my story. It cost me to write it, to wade back into the seas of grief after I'd just swam them. To share the most vulnerable and tender parts of my grief in such a transparent way. Yet there was no way I couldn't write it—I needed to build a temple for those experiences, and a place to honor Brent. Now they will forever reside inside of that book, reaching out and through and touching others who are working on building their own temples to honor those they've lost.

And somebody has seen the value in that, they thought it was good enough for a Silver, and it undoes me.

I went to Sleeping Giant earlier today to try and ground and get a grip on myself. I can tell Brent is waiting at the top, I just feel it this day. He feels close by already and there's something about the peace and calm and perspective of a mountaintop that makes it easier to feel and hear him, which is why he usually waits until I've ascended and settled onto my favorite perch to try and reach me.

As soon as I sit down and press my hand on my heart I see him in his brightness; not as he used to appear to me, when he still looked more human in my heart's eye, but as a light being.

Big and beautiful, once again he's surrounded by angelic presence. Emerald and sapphire and ruby and amethyst lights stream down on me. Golds and pinks and silvers and shimmers. Wings and feathers and bells and chimes. It's a dance and shower of love, and I sit in the middle and weep, humbled, unraveled, overcome.

It doesn't last long, just long enough to feel God-swept, rainbow-wrapped, congratulated, blessed. Brent and the angels are soon gone, and it's just me left alone with my thoughts. Just me returning to the space of myself. Sitting up high above the jungle green. Looking out at the world below with love.

Taking the hand of my younger self, that girl in 2016 who so bravely journeyed through the land of grief with such naked honesty and vulnerability, and telling her: *I am so proud of you. So, so proud. Thank you for helping me reach this place today.*

Then I take her down off the mountain and between more bouts of tears and laughter, make her a cup of celebratory cocoa and sit down to keep on writing.

119

Finding BethAnne

Sunset's violet tones, peach streaks, and pink clouds tell a tale of May's sky. The sun is out longer and hotter, the humidity is high, and the weather gives me a sense of nostalgia and remembrance of last summer when we first arrived on the island.

Much has happened in a year, a lot of internal rearrangement has occurred, and I am beginning to feel a deeper sense of integration that has taken place. A sediment and cementing that has helped me have a more profound sense of self.

I realize now that when I first got to this island I was hoping somebody would come along beside me and help me figure *me* out. As I reflect, it strikes me that was a ridiculous notion. As if somebody else could tell me more about me than I can. As if somebody else knows my soul better than I know my soul. I've realized since I've been over here that my God given work is to know my soul. And to claim it. Others may act as a catalyst for greater knowing, but my highest library of information is inside.

It's taken me a while to put my pieces back together in Kauai. This time last year, I was deconstructing my Alaskan life in preparation to move to this island. I didn't know if I wanted to be a psychologist anymore, I had a massive solitude wound which was suffering from too much busyness, obligation, responsibility, and otherness. I knew I had creative and spiritual gifts trying to surface, but I couldn't quite see the where or how.

Reconstruction hasn't always gone as planned. I expected my path to manifest quicker than it did, and now I see this first year has been an incubation period where I have had the gift of space and germination and time to come to terms with a fuller version of myself. And time to grieve; I still have bits and pieces of shrapnel from the loss of my brother that surprise me with their intensity.

Even though I was initially impatient when I got here, I see now time has been my friend, and many things have changed in my life in a year's time.

A year ago, I finally wrote a post on my website about sensing my brother in the afterlife and the gifts that opened up in my life after he passed. I was so nervous at the time, I felt like I was spiritually coming out of the closet. And yet there was liberation there too—I had a whole other side of my story I hadn't been telling, and when stories sit inside of you too long they become heavy and they alienate.

Untold stories make you feel like you don't belong.

I don't like labels—they are constrictive and often create a lens of perception that has judgment and expectation attached. Yet we have to use language to describe our experiences the best we know how. When I first started writing and talking about these things, I didn't know what to call myself or my gifts. I grabbed at language the best I could. An Intuitive. A Mystic. A Psychic. Angel Talker. Worlds Walker. Channeler.

And now I've come to realize, that all words fall so short and flat. My experience of Self and with Spirit is so transdimensional and multidimensional. These experiences have become a part of who I am, they are not separate from me—meant to be labeled in boxes and kept in a closet, only taken out around those who believe such things.

They are who I'm created to be.

So I can embody them and grow in them and walk a deeper path of love, peace, and grace. And the freedom and grace that has come from living in Kauai have given me space to own them, claim them, and embody them in greater ways.

I'm so profoundly grateful for that, as I have more clearly seen in the process of writing this book that part of me was suffocating inside. She didn't have enough space to breathe and let her lungs expand or find her wingspan. She craves solitude and nature and time in daydream, so she can connect with things beyond herself. Back in Alaska, she didn't feel particularly valued, understood, or seen for the most beautiful, sensitive, perceptive parts of herself. *Now, here in Kauai, I've realized that all along it was simply me who needed to value, understand, and see me.*

We have to learn to be our own best friend in this life. Because when we become our own best friend, we begin to give ourselves permission to live in such a way that our lives become deeper and richer as our experience of self is always validated, appreciated, and loved.

It's taken me a while to catch up with myself, to shrug off what others may think, and just be me without excuse or explanation or defense or presentation. But somewhere along the timeline from last year until now, I've stepped into my self and the woman I needed to be.

And I like her. She's not afraid anymore. She doesn't have to be kept hidden.

She is living what it means to be free.

120

Wild Flowers

S URROUND YOURSELF WITH whatever brings out the *real* in you. Fostering love and truth in your life will help you foster love and truth in yourself. Be a student and allow nature to be your teacher. Talk to the stars, listen for their answer echoing in your soul. See shapes in the clouds and dragons in crowds of swaying trees. Believe in magic and mystery.

Remember the ancestors who walked here first, know that we step where they once trod and now rest. Know that all land and ground is sacred. Reestablish a connection with it. Learn to set your heart beat to the beat of the bones of the earth. Learn to beat as one. Learn what true connection means.

Stay away from people and places that tear you down. Don't change your shape to fit any boxes that don't suit your glorious bursts of sunlight, sky, and sea. Realize your experience of self is right and real and worthy. Realize your experience of life is the only experience that is going to be most helpful to you.

Don't wait if it's in your heart to do and you have the means to do it Now. Become a waking dream. See the world through rose-colored lens. Create a beautiful reality.

Grieve as often as your spirit requires over the cracks and ruptures in this place, let your heart break daily if need be, make up your own sacred ceremonies to honor the pains that you feel and see. But don't let this hurting world make you forget that the healing and binding balm of LOVE unleashed far surpasses everything.

Pull anything into you that encourages, supports, and nourishes you into bloom like the gorgeous, mad, wild flower that you are. Grow and keep growing and grow some more—until your roots are bound in the ruby of the earth and your platinum petals reach up, up, up to Pleiades, forming their own milky way galaxies.

Become so BIG you can't ever go back to small.

121

A Thousand Comets

My dear one,
don't let them dull your glow.
Not everybody can stand
the sight of bright sunlight
or a thousand comets racing
through night's sky.

And you are the sun
and the moon at its fullest
blazing so bright—
it comes into your window at night,
waking you with its force.
And you my dear one,
(yes you)
you are a force to be reckoned.

So do not let them pull
you down or take from you
your birthright—

Which was given to you
to claim your space
and shine the full force
of your blinding heartlight.

122

HIS BRIGHT LIGHT

THERE IS A sense of change hanging in the misty jungle air. I'm saying goodbye to something, and I don't even know what, but I can feel a deeper sense of letting go echoing in my heart and bones. I have a sense of closing a chapter and completing a cycle, even as there are twinklings and inklings that a new cycle is about to begin.

I can't see what that is; I can feel it though. And I trust my feelings. Even if I can't always see the logic in them, I've learned that my feelings are my gateway to my higher self and my heart and my intuition. When they get stirred in premonition there is always a reason, as my soul is once again preparing me for whatever is waiting around the corner. I have the sense that my ongoing question of "what next" is going to soon be answered, and I'll have illumination for the next step on my path.

Isn't it strange how much can change in our inside worlds, even if it appears nothing has changed outside of us. Something is different, Kauai life resumes as usual, yet I keep getting a felt-sense of spiraling deeper; experiencing my own sense of self and truth in a new way.

Brent feels like he's changed. Ever since I called him and caught a glimpse of who and where he is now, I haven't felt him in the same way I used to. Just like when I first became aware of his presence those few days after his death, and I explained it as a new musical composition being introduced into my stream of consciousness, the music has shifted.

It feels bigger and brighter now. Different than before.

And Brent feels bigger and brighter and different than he was before. I can't tell if he's changed or my perspective of him has changed—maybe it's a little of both. He has a new life on the other side, it makes sense that he should and would experience change as a soul, as he keeps journeying on and growing in other realms.

Even as I keep changing and growing down here.

My husband and I are different too. This last season shook us up and out and turned us upside down, and the old contents we once organized ourselves around that gave us a sense of "us" have been reorganized and reworked. More mercy exists. A more expansive love. A deeper understanding of personhood. A deeper awareness of where we intersect and where we are each on our own soul journey.

My family feels different too. There is a gentleness and a smoothing over of the past that has taken place between my parents. Grief unpacked and decluttered the things that no longer matter. Moving permanently to the island is their last step and stop in their golden years, and that leaves us with an awareness that the memories we make moving forward are finite and precious.

Maybe that's just what this island does to you if you live on her long enough. Deepens your awareness. Brings broken pieces to the surface so they can be polished and rubbed and softened. Teaches you patience in the process. Continues to reveal new mysteries to you with her own sense of timing and revelation; just when you think you are beginning to understand, things shift and new mysteries begin to unlock and open up.

Like Brent.

I've been thinking a great deal about what he showed me when he gave me the pictures of the child's model of the solar system and the actual solar system. One a mere representation, the other the miracle of the cosmos. When I take that thought process one step further, I imagine the difference between gazing at the stars and planets of the cosmos compared to actually traveling to them.

What if each of us could fly up and experience the miracle instead of just contemplating it? How much bigger, how much vaster, how much more astonishing, magical, and awesome would that be?

That is Brent now. That's what he was trying to show me, my mind is just limited in how it can grasp it. Maybe Brent continues to change but so does my own perception, and as that perspective shifts, how he's coming through to me also shifts. Like changing the lens on your glasses; my lens is changing. *Or maybe I'm just taking off my glasses.*

It's as if Brent had been translating himself to me in ways that I could understand; ways that make sense to my limited human consciousness, which helped me recognize Brent for Brent. In some ways he's been what I needed him to be during this time, still coming to me in a manner I humanly connect with. But he's no longer human, he's divine light, he exists on another realm, and there's so much more to him and his story and his soul than what he's shown me.

And now that I'm beginning to shift and grow in my own perceptions and consciousness, I can feel Brent knows it and he's going to start translating differently.

We're not in Beginners Spanish anymore Little Sister, we've graduated to Intermediate. You don't need the basics, get ready to learn something new. I'm still here, but it's going to be different.

The words bring me pause. I've had an expectation of how he is going to show up, and now it occurs to me that once again I'm being asked to release expectation. I'm being asked to release how I think it's going to look, so I can better see how it does look. I've read numerous accounts of other people who've had contact with their loved one in the afterlife, I thought that was going to be our story as well, but what if Brent is trying to translate a different story?

Maybe that's why he feels so different. Because *this* is different. And it's going to be different than anything I've read about or thought about or imagined.

I suddenly have the sense that the training wheels just popped off my bicycle, and I didn't even know they were there. There is a loss in the stability and familiarity of those wheels, and I find myself nostalgically and wistfully saying goodbye to younger things, even as I have a surge of expectation for what will happen now that I've learned to fully ride a bike.

Surging forward. *Pedaling, pedaling, pedaling* beneath the transformative sun, moving towards something I still can't see but is undeniably drawing me.

Somewhere in another realm, I can sense Brent on a parallel journey doing the same, smiling. I pedal even harder beneath the grace of his bright light.

AFTERWARDS AND UPWARDS

WE HAVE TO learn to become our own truth tellers. That is my biggest takeaway from writing *Transformations*, where I found the words poured out of me so fast I had a hard time keeping up at times. I didn't realize just how much the sparks of this story were trying to ignite until I let those flames out, set them free on page, and watched them burn away everything but my deepest truth.

As always, my truth brought me back to *Love*. Love for my brother. Love for this beautiful world I'm so grateful to belong to. Love for Spirit. Love for others. Love for myself. And I realized that as somebody who lives life from the inside out and seeks to live in such a way as to walk a path of authenticity, that keeping quiet about Brent and Spirit and all that transpired in these pages would be an act of fear. And acts of fear are acts of unlove. And that is not who I wish to be in this world.

Speaking of love, I need to spread a little around with a few thank yous: Thank you to Anita Neilson for reviewing this book in advance and lending your golden words of support. Thank you to Carolyn Riker for being an encouragement, support, and sounding board for the whole of this project and for thinking of and gifting me with the term "transcendental psychology." And last, but not the least bit least, my sincerest gratitude to Alice Maldonado at Golden Dragonfly Press for publishing my work and continuing to see the value in my words.

A few notes and credits: *Infinity* was previously published in *Heliotrope Nights* (Golden Dragonfly Press, 2017). *Weather Patterns* was previously published in *Heliotrope Nights* (Golden Dragonfly Press, 2017). The original version of *Duckpond* was published in *freebird fridays* (Golden Dragonfly Press, 2016). *Ouroboros* was originally published through *The Urban Howl*. *How To Know Your Soul* was previously published in *Heliotrope Nights* (Golden Dragonfly Press, 2017).

The reference to Rumi's field in the piece *Spirit* is inspired by his quote, "Out beyond ideas of wrongdoing and rightdoing there is a field. I'll meet you there. When the soul lies down in that grass, the world is too full to talk about." The reference to Mele Kalikimaka at the end of *Christmas Ornaments* is inspired by the lyrics of Bing Crosby. The quote used in *Here At The End of All Things* is from J.R.R. Tolkien's *Return of The King*. The lyrics quoted in *I'm A Rainbow Too* are from Bob Marley's *Sun is Shining*. The phrase "collateral beauty" in *Pennies*, is inspired by the movie title *Collateral Beauty*. In *Finding Brent*, the lyrics to *Lean on Me* are sung by *Bill Withers*, and the reference to Harry Potter and his liquid luck is from J.K. Rowling's, *Harry Potter and The Half Blood Prince*. The reference to *take me home country roads* in *Remember What Was Best In Us* is from John Denver's *Country Roads*.

If my intuition serves me correct, there is at least another book on the way in this series. Possibly a few more—I couldn't say for sure as I haven't lived those moments yet—I write my experiences as I go, and if/when another book says "I'm ready!" then I'll know it's time. In the meantime, Brent seems like he has more to share, and those angels keep showing up in bigger and brighter ways, and by the time this book is released I'll be in my "sophomore year" on the island of Kauai, and so I expect there's a lot of new, beautiful, and very human lessons around the corner as I live my own question of "what next" and find my answers through the experience of living.

Last, If you have made it this far and joined me for this journey then I bless you and thank you and send love, joy, and beauty to you and your magnificent heart. May we all keep learning and growing and grieving and healing and coming together and being the love we need.

Love,
BethAnne

About the Author

Dr. BethAnne K.W. is a psychologist, intuitive, creative, and writer living on the magical island of Kauai. She specializes in grief work; creativity and being; personal artistry and spirituality; supporting others in finding their soul calling; and transcendental psychology, a multi-dimensional approach to healing.

She is the award-winning author of *Lamentations of The Sea: 111 passages on grief, love, loss, and letting go*. She also writes and illustrates books for all ages. Color nurtures her soul. She is currently working on a series of children's books inspired by her best muse, her fur kids. She published several poetry books: *freebird fridays, Heliotrope Nights,* and *Cranberry Dusk*.

www.bethannekw.blog

Made in the USA
Columbia, SC
19 July 2022

63712304R00143